Fast Facts: Psychiatry Highlights 2005–06
First published March 2006

© 2006 in this edition Health Press Limited
Health Press Limited, Elizabeth House, Queen Street, Abingdon,
Oxford OX14 3LN, UK
Tel: +44 (0)1235 523233
Fax: +44 (0)1235 523238

Book orders can be placed by telephone or via the website.
For regional distributors or to order via the website, please go to:
www.fastfacts.com
For telephone orders, please call 01752 202301 (UK), +44 1752 202301 (Europe),
1 800 247 6553 (USA, toll free) or +1 419 281 1802 (Americas).

Fast Facts is a trademark of Health Press Limited.

A CIP record for this title is available from the British Library.

ISBN 1-903734-85-1

Lader, M (Malcolm)
Fast Facts: Psychiatry Highlights 2005–06/
Malcolm Lader

Typesetting and page layout by Zed, Oxford, UK.
Printed by Fine Print (Services) Ltd, Oxford, UK.

Printed with vegetable inks on fully biodegradable and
recyclable paper manufactured from sustainable forests.

444   001

Low emissions
during production

Low
chlorine

Sustainable
forests

Introduction

This is the third edition of *Fast Facts: Psychiatry Highlights*. The previous two have proved most popular as a brief update on topics that have attracted much interest in the recent past. The format allows an intense but brief study of quite complex topics that are rapidly evolving. The readership seems to be quite wide, encompassing busy clinicians and academic scientists.

The 11 chapters in this edition cover a wide range of concepts, mostly theoretical but also in highly practical areas. Under the first rubric are chapters on the 'Classification of depressive disorders' and on 'What is "theory of mind"?'. The relationship between psychiatric and physical disorders is the substance of the chapters on 'Depression and ischemic heart disease' and 'The physical health of people with schizophrenia', while 'Hoarding' deals with the content of psychiatric illness. 'Suicide in China' and 'Major mental disorders and homicide' cover two important consequences of psychiatric disorders. Finally, therapy is the subject of the chapters on 'Treatment of behavioral symptoms in the dementias', 'Treatment of obsessive–compulsive disorder', 'Psychotherapies in treatment-resistant depression' and 'Benzodiazepine use and cognitive decline'.

The format is as before, with the emphasis on updating the reader with respect to changes in theory and practice, in particular any accrual of research data that has modified the evidence-based nature of our knowledge and opinions. All the contributors are international experts in their field. I thank them for finding the time to provide such authoritative and comprehensive yet succinct reviews.

Malcolm Lader OBE DSc PhD MD FRCPsych FMedSci
Emeritus Professor of Clinical Psychopharmacology
Institute of Psychiatry
King's College London, UK

Classification of depressive disorders

Gordon Parker MB BS MD PhD DSc UNSW FRANZCP
Black Dog Institute, Sydney, Australia

For a long time, academic psychiatrists were preoccupied as to whether depression was best modeled as a unitary condition (i.e. a single entity, varying only dimensionally in severity, duration and persistence) or according to a binary model (i.e. 'endogenous' versus 'reactive' disorders, with life events respectively being either irrelevant or determining).

The concept of an 'endogenous' disorder became untenable when studies established life-event stressors as antecedents to each 'type' of depression. 'Endogenous' depression was therefore informally replaced by 'melancholic' depression to describe the quintessential biological depressive subtype.

Historically, the melancholic subtype has been held to have multiple defining characteristics, including:

- a distinctive pattern of symptoms and signs (e.g. psychomotor disturbance, non-reactive mood and anhedonia)
- a greater relevance of genetic and other biological determinants
- concomitant evidence of disturbed biological functioning (e.g. the hypothalamic–pituitary–adrenal axis)
- selective responses to physical treatments such as antidepressant medications and electroconvulsive therapy (ECT).

In reality, the non-melancholic disorders do not form a pure type. Instead, they reflect a heterogeneous residue of multiple differing expressions of depression. These residual disorders have no specific characteristics, apart from the absence of melancholic features.

The unitary versus binary debate was largely made irrelevant by the publication of the third edition of the *Diagnostic and Statistical Manual of Mental Disorders* (DSM-III) 25 years ago. In essence, DSM-III posited a primary dimensional, symptom-based and non-causal model, comprising 'major depression' and 'minor depressive' disorders. For those meeting the criteria for major depression, subsidiary diagnoses, such as 'melancholia' or 'depression with psychotic features', could be applied, although the criteria set for melancholia differ little from the base diagnosis of major depression and have problematic validity.

Non-specific classification

Major depression has progressively become refined as an entity. However, a diagnosis of major depression has proved relatively meaningless in terms of its relevance to research and management.[1,2] No consistent etiology has been identified, as might be anticipated for a heterogeneous group.

Randomized controlled treatment trials of patients with major depression tend to show similar rates of efficacy for differing antidepressant drugs, differing psychotherapies and even St John's wort. Such trials provide a non-specific result for a non-specific diagnosis, minimizing therapeutic attention to cause, and advancing an 'all roads lead to Rome' treatment model. Such a non-specific classification runs the risk of patients being 'fitted' to the therapist's paradigm rather than treatment being 'fitted' to the particular depressive disorder.

The problem of non-specific classification can be better explained using the analogy of 'major breathlessness'.[1] This categorization is minimally informative and provides only a first-level diagnosis. It requires further subtyping with respect to etiology (e.g. asthma, pneumonia or pulmonary embolism), so that the appropriate treatment (e.g. bronchodilator, antibiotic or anticoagulant) can then be rationally derived.

A macro-hierarchical model

Although many researchers still argue for a unitary or continuum model,[3] or for an etiology-based distinction (as illustrated by vascular depression),[4] perhaps multiple models are required given that depression can be a disease, a disorder or even considered 'normal'.

Specifically, a macro-hierarchical model (Figure 1) can be used to conceptualize the principal depressive classes, that is:

- psychotic depression
- melancholic depression
- residual non-melancholic disorders.

All three – as depressive disorders – have a central 'depressive mood' component, which differs in overall severity but not sufficiently to aid overall definition. The definition of melancholia relies on the presence of observable psychomotor disturbance (PMD) (i.e. retardation, agitation and cognitive processing difficulties), which gives it a phenotypic weighting. PMD is even more severe in psychotic depression, but in this case the diagnosis can be made from the specific presence of psychotic features (delusions and/or hallucinations), again providing a phenotypic weighting.

A 'functional model' can be used to show the different contributions made by three principal neurotransmitter systems to the three depressive classes (see Figure 1).[5] Thus, for the non-melancholic disorders, the principal perturbation is assumed to be the serotonergic system. For melancholic depression, there is a greater noradrenergic contribution, and for psychotic depression there is a greater dopaminergic contribution. If valid, this working hypothesis provides a more rational model for antidepressant drug

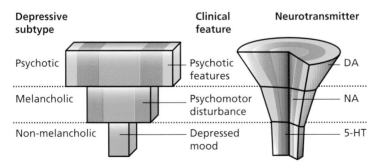

Figure 1 A model based on the structural and functional components of the three main depressive classes, showing the contribution made by three principal neurotransmitter systems. DA, dopaminergic; NA, noradrenergic; 5-HT, serotonergic. Reproduced from Malhi et al.[5] with permission of Blackwell.

selection. The model suggests that for non-melancholic disorders, all antidepressant classes might have similar efficacy; for melancholic depression, dual-action antidepressants would (overall) have greater efficacy than selective serotonergic drugs; and for psychotic depression, a broad-spectrum approach (e.g. a combination of antipsychotic and antidepressant drugs) would be required.

The influence of personality style

The spectrum model for non-melancholic disorders shown in Figure 2 principally reflects severe and salient life-event stresses acting alone or in interaction with the individual's personality style. It identifies a number of at-risk personality styles (e.g. anxious worrying, shy, sensitive to rejection).[2]

The clinical or phenotypic picture of the non-melancholic disorders can – to some degree – be influenced by the underlying personality style. For example, underlying personality traits

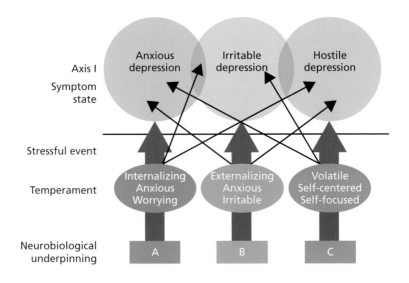

Figure 2 Spectrum model for non-melancholic depression. Originally produced in Parker G, Manicavasagar V. *Modelling and Managing the Depressive Disorders: A Clinical Guide.* Cambridge; New York: Cambridge University Press, 2005:83.

(e.g. anxious worrying) dispose the individual to depression under certain circumstances and, to a variable degree, shape the clinical picture (in this case, 'anxious depression').

Those who externalize an anxious personality style are more likely to have 'irritable depression', while those with a volatile personality will be more likely to present clinically with 'hostile depression'. However, as the effects of personality style and life stresses are dimensional, their clinical characterization is less clear-cut than for the melancholic and psychotic disorders, so that a diathesis–stress model should be favored over any phenotypic pattern.

Etiologic weighting

McHugh has argued recently for a classification system that weights 'etiopathic' groups.[6] Three of the four he described have relevance to the depressive disorders. First, certain brain diseases that 'directly disrupt neural underpinnings of psychological faculties'; second, patients who are 'vulnerable to mental unrest because of their psychological makeup', giving greater weighting to predisposing factors such as personality style rather than the stressor; and third, patients who have 'distressing mental conditions provoked by events thwarting or endangering their hopes', a model that gives greater weighting to the stressor, acute or chronic. Melancholic depression is an appropriate example of the first etiopathic group, while the last two are relevant to the non-melancholic disorders.

Further refinement

As phenomenological distinctions have varying relevance to carving the depressive disorders 'at their joints' and etiologic models are compromised by putative causal events having diffuse outcomes, each of these bases for classification is, in itself, unsatisfactory. There is, therefore, wisdom in pursuing a classification system by progressively refining (using iterative research) a model that weights both phenomenology and cause, to create 'thick descriptions' as have proved satisfactory to anthropological interpretation.

Highlights *in* classification of depressive disorders *2005–06*

WHAT'S IN?

- A realization that efficacy data for differing antidepressant treatments from randomized controlled trials (RCTs) are of little relevance to the clinician because of their lack of specificity, underpinned (in part) by a non-specific dimensional model for classifying the depressive disorders

- Concern that antidepressant drugs differ little from placebo in formal RCTs, again reflecting (in part) treatments being tested against non-specific depressive categories (e.g. major depression, dysthymia), and as if they have universal application

WHAT'S NEEDED?

- Significant debate about the importance of classification of depressive disorders

References

1. Parker G. Beyond major depression. *Psychol Med* 2005;35: 467–74.

2. Parker G, Manicavasagar V. *Modelling and Managing the Depressive Disorders. A Clinical Guide*. Cambridge; New York: Cambridge University Press, 2005.

3. Angst J, Merikangas KR. Multi-dimensional criteria for the diagnosis of depression. *J Affect Disord* 2001; 62:7–15.

4. Baldwin RC. Is vascular depression a distinct sub-type of depressive disorder? A review of causal evidence. *Int J Geriatr Psychiatry* 2005;20: 1–11.

5. Malhi GS, Parker GB, Greenwood J. Structural and functional models of depression: from sub-types to substrates. *Acta Psychiatr Scand* 2005;111:94–105.

6. McHugh PR. Striving for coherence: psychiatry's efforts over classification. *JAMA* 2005;293: 2526–8.

Depression and ischemic heart disease

Claus Havregaard Sørensen* MD and Per Bech[†] MD

*Department of Psychiatry, Odense University Hospital, Odense, Denmark
[†]Psychiatric Research Unit, Frederiksborg General Hospital, Hillerød, Denmark

Epidemiology

It is almost 70 years since the publication of the first report that showed an increased risk of mortality due to cardiovascular disease (CVD) in patients with depressive illness.[1] In the report, the mortality risk due to CVD was estimated to be approximately nine times higher than that in the general population. Since then, however, epidemiological studies have found that the relative risk (RR) of mortality due to CVD in depressed patients is, in fact, around two times higher than that in the general population.[2–4] For example, subjects in a general population study who were identified as being depressed had an RR of around 2 for developing ischemic heart disease (IHD) when followed up years later.[4]

The prevalence of depression in patients with myocardial infarction (MI) was found to be 30–50% when investigators screened study participants using questionnaires, but only 2–20% when they assessed participants by interview on the basis of the diagnosis for major depression detailed in the fourth edition of the *Diagnostic and Statistical Manual of Mental Disorders* (DSM-IV).

Pathophysiology

Researchers have repeatedly shown that depression is associated with hyperactivity of the hypothalamic–pituitary–adrenal axis, resulting in hypercortisolemia.[5] Hypercortisolemia is associated with hypertension, hypercholesterolemia, hypertriglyceridemia and impaired glucose tolerance, all well-known risk factors for atherosclerosis.[6] The inflammatory response to damaged, atherosclerotic, arterial endothelial cells results in increased levels of inflammatory markers such as C-reactive protein, interleukin-6

13

and tumor necrosis factor-α, all of which have been associated with IHD. Patients with depression have high levels of these markers – approximately 25–40% higher levels than in individuals from the background population.[7]

Elevated levels of catecholamines, indicating increased activity of the sympathetic nervous system, have also been found in patients with depression.[8] Raised levels of catecholamines have been associated with recurrent endothelial injury and thereby with atherosclerosis. Furthermore, elevated levels of catecholamines have been associated with an increased heart rate.[8] Heart rate variability (HRV), which is a measure of the balance between the sympathetic and parasympathetic systems' control of cardiac rhythm, is lower in patients with depression.[9] Diminished HRV predisposes to cardiac arrhythmias and thereby to sudden death. HRV has been found to be significantly lower in depressed patients with IHD than in non-depressed patients with IHD.[10]

In addition, elevated levels of catecholamines potentiate platelet activation, and may cause platelet aggregation.[11] Activation and aggregation of platelets are key elements in acute manifestations of IHD such as MI and unstable angina pectoris (UAP). In depressed patients, platelet activation is increased, with higher pro-coagulant properties than in non-depressed controls.[12] The same has been found in depressed post-MI patients compared with non-depressed MI patients.[13]

Treatment

Pharmacological. A feature of depression is the depletion of serotonin, not only in the brain but also in the platelets, causing an increased expression of serotonin receptors and subsequent binding of serotonin to the platelets.[14] Treatment with a selective serotonin-reuptake inhibitor (SSRI) reduces platelet activation in depressed post-MI patients.[15] A recent study showed that SSRI treatment reduces the risk of reinfarction and death in depressed post-MI patients.[16]

So far, data from two large-scale treatment trials have been reported: SADHART[17] and ENRICHD.[18] In the SADHART trial,

Highlights in **depression and ischemic heart disease** *2005–06*

WHAT'S IN?

- Agreement that depressed patients have a relative risk of approximately 1.5–2 of ischemic heart disease (IHD) and mortality

- Awareness that the physiological consequences of depression (including hypercortisolemia, chronic elevated inflammatory markers and elevated levels of catecholamines) may increase the risk of IHD

- Prediction of depression in patients after myocardial infarction (MI) by risk factors for depression, not by cardiovascular risk factors

WHAT'S NEW?

- Treatment of depression with selective serotonin-reuptake inhibitors (SSRIs) in post-MI patients, reducing mortality and risk of reinfarction, most likely by decreasing platelet activation

WHAT'S NEEDED?

- Better identification of subgroups with an increased risk for mortality after MI

- Randomized controlled trials with an SSRI in a subgroup of depressed post-MI patients with increased risk of mortality

- Long-term follow-up studies to examine if an increased risk of mortality persists after treatment

patients with major depression after MI or UAP were randomized to the SSRI sertraline or placebo. The trial was intended to assess efficacy, but mortality was a secondary endpoint. There was no statistically significant difference in mortality between the two

15

groups. In the ENRICHD study, patients with depression and/or low social support were randomized to either cognitive behavioral therapy and SSRI treatment, if severely depressed, or treatment as usual. There was no difference in mortality between the two groups. However, secondary analysis of patients participating in the ENRICHD study showed that the use of SSRIs was related to a lower rate of reinfarction or death, most likely reflecting an effect on platelet function, as described above.[16]

Post-hoc power calculations of the SADHART results indicate that 4000 post-MI/UAP patients with major depression should have been included to obtain a statistical difference of 20% for serious cardiovascular events between patients receiving sertraline and placebo. This makes future studies very large and extremely expensive; therefore we must improve our identification of patients at increased risk of death after MI/UAP and optimize interventions in specific subgroups.

Non-pharmacological. Depression is often associated with passive coping mechanisms, such as low motor activity, sedentary behavior and the use of psychoactive substances such as tobacco and alcohol,[19] all of which are also major factors in the development of coronary heart disease.[20] Health professionals have an important role in helping patients with depression to reduce their reliance on these coping mechanisms and hence reduce the risk of heart disease.

References

1. Malzberg B. Mortality among patients with involution melancholia. *Am J Psychiatry* 1937;93:1231–8.

2. Hoyer EH, Mortensen PB, Olesen AV. Mortality and causes of death in a total national sample of patients with affective disorders admitted for the first time between 1973 and 1993. *Br J Psychiatry* 2000;176:76–82.

3. Sørensen C, Friis-Hasché E, Haghfelt T, Bech P. Postmyocardial infarction mortality in relation to depression: a systematic critical review. *Psychother Psychosom* 2005;74:69–80.

4. Ladwig KH, Marten-Mittag B, Lowel H et al. C-reactive protein, depressed mood, and the prediction of coronary heart disease in initially healthy men: results from the MONICA-KORA Augsburg Cohort Study 1984–1998. *Eur Heart J* 2005;26:2537–42.

5. Barden N. Implication of the hypothalamic-pituitary-adrenal axis in the pathophysiology of depression. *J Psychiatry Neurosci* 2004;29: 185–93.

6. Girod JP, Brotman DJ. Does altered glucocorticoid homeostasis increase cardiovascular risk? *Cardiovasc Res* 2004;64:217–26.

7. Empana JP, Sykes DH, Luc G et al. Contributions of depressive mood and circulating inflammatory markers to coronary heart disease in healthy European men: the Prospective Epidemiological Study of Myocardial Infarction (PRIME). *Circulation* 2005;111:2299–305.

8. Veith RC, Lewis N, Linares OA et al. Sympathetic nervous system activity in major depression. Basal and desipramine-induced alterations in plasma norepinephrine kinetics. *Arch Gen Psychiatry* 1994;51: 411–22.

9. Rechlin T, Weis M, Spitzer A, Kaschka WP. Are affective disorders associated with alterations of heart rate variability? *J Affect Disord* 1994;32:271–5.

10. Carney RM, Saunders RD, Freedland KE et al. Association of depression with reduced heart rate variability in coronary artery disease. *Am J Cardiol* 1995;76:562–4.

11. Musselman DL, Evans DL, Nemeroff CB. The relationship of depression to cardiovascular disease: epidemiology, biology, and treatment. *Arch Gen Psychiatry* 1998;55: 580–92.

12. Musselman DL, Tomer A, Manatunga AK et al. Exaggerated platelet reactivity in major depression. *Am J Psychiatry* 1996; 153:1313–7.

13. Kuijpers PM, Hamulyak K, Strik JJ et al. Beta-thromboglobulin and platelet factor 4 levels in post-myocardial infarction patients with major depression. *Psychiatry Res* 2002;109:207–10.

14. Mendelson SD. The current status of the platelet 5-HT(2A) receptor in depression. *J Affect Disord* 2000;57: 13–24.

15. Serebruany VL, Suckow RF, Cooper TB et al. Relationship between release of platelet/endothelial biomarkers and plasma levels of sertraline and N-desmethylsertraline in acute coronary syndrome patients receiving SSRI treatment for depression. *Am J Psychiatry* 2005; 162:1165–70.

16. Taylor CB, Youngblood ME, Catellier D et al. Effects of antidepressant medication on morbidity and mortality in depressed patients after myocardial infarction. *Arch Gen Psychiatry* 2005;62:792–8.

17. Glassman AH, O'Connor CM, Califf RM et al. Sertraline treatment of major depression in patients with acute MI or unstable angina. *JAMA* 2002;288:701–9.

18. Berkman LF, Blumenthal J, Burg M et al.; ENRICHD investigators. Effects of treating depression and low perceived social support on clinical events after myocardial infarction: the Enhancing Recovery in Coronary Heart Disease Patients (ENRICHD) Randomized Trial. *JAMA* 2003;289: 3106–16.

19. Bech P, Andersen MB, Bech-Andersen G et al. Work-related stressors, depression and quality of life in Danish managers. *Eur Psychiatry* 2005;(suppl 3):S318–25.

20. Brummett BH, Babyak MA, Siegler IC et al. Effect of smoking and sedentary behavior on the association between depressive symptoms and mortality from coronary heart disease. *Am J Cardiol* 2003;92: 529–32.

Treatment of behavioral symptoms in the dementias

Myron F Weiner MD

University of Texas Southwestern Medical Center, Dallas, Texas, USA

Behavioral symptoms are common in individuals with dementias. They include apathy, depression, anxiety, suspicion, psychotic symptoms, sleep–wake disturbances, 'shadowing' of caregivers, wandering, and a group of unrelated behaviors lumped together as 'agitation', which include physical and verbal aggression that may or may not have a specific aim or object.[1]

Whether or not any of these symptoms is seen as a problem depends on the context in which they arise, and whether interpersonal relationships and the physical environment can be adapted to meet the patient's ever-changing needs for structure and non-intrusive support and supervision. For example, apathy or the loss of initiative in an individual with early Alzheimer's disease or a frontotemporal dementia is considered problematic by family members when the person is living at home and part of a larger social network. Loss of initiative among more severely demented people living in long-term care facilities is often not seen as a problem, because it lessens the onus on staff to redirect them from wandering into others' rooms or attempting to escape from the facility.

Depression

Major depression in patients with dementia responds to conventional antidepressant therapy.[2] Because the drugs currently in use (e.g. selective serotonin-reuptake inhibitors) have relatively benign side-effect profiles, it seems appropriate that clinicians treat at the first suspicion of depression, rather than waiting for a full-blown episode to emerge. It is important to recognize that, as in children, increased irritability may be the predominant symptom of depression in patients with dementia.

Psychotic symptoms

Because psychotic symptoms in dementia patients tend to be transient, it has been difficult to assess their treatment. In general, antipsychotic agents appear to be weakly effective for these symptoms and their associated behavioral disturbances.[3] Atypical agents should be used with caution in elderly people because of a reported increased risk of vascular events.[4] In addition, low-potency typical antipsychotics should be avoided because of their cardiotoxicity.

Frequent, disturbing visual hallucinations in individuals with dementing illness (in the absence of delirium) suggest dementia with Lewy bodies. These patients may respond to a cholinesterase inhibitor[5] or to quetiapine,[6] an atypical antipsychotic with little propensity for producing extrapyramidal symptoms.

Anxiety

Dementia patients who complain of anxiety may be treated behaviorally (by reassurance) or pharmacologically, but there are no randomized controlled trials to guide treatment for this symptom.

In general, benzodiazepines are avoided in elderly people because they tend to cause confusion and falls, but low oral doses of a short-acting drug (e.g. lorazepam, 0.5 mg) are frequently employed. Other medications administered for anxiety include once- or twice-daily low doses of haloperidol (0.5 mg) or risperidone (0.25–0.5 mg), or twice- or thrice-daily doses of trazodone (25–50 mg).

Sleep–wake disturbances

Sleep–wake disturbances, such as sleeping during the day with frequent arousals at night, can be dealt with effectively by sleep hygiene measures. These include keeping active during the day and increased exposure to light.[7]

Although there are few controlled trials to guide treatment regimens, agents frequently employed for night-time sedation are oral doses of trazodone, 50–100 mg, mirtazepine, 15–30 mg, or quetiapine, 25–50 mg.

Other behavioral symptoms

Symptoms of shadowing, wandering, pacing, rummaging, and verbal or physical aggression (including irritability) may be regarded as a dysexecutive syndrome (dysfunction in flexibility, sequencing and planning ahead) or a disinhibition syndrome (characterized by poor impulse control, explosive outbursts, verbal lewdness or a lack of interpersonal sensitivity). The basic management for these types of syndrome is the creation of a tolerant, supportive environment, including the provision of a safe place to rummage, pace and wander.

Verbal and physical aggression are best dealt with by trying to reduce environmental triggers; for example, caregivers may attempt to correct patients' misperceptions or denial of their impairment.[1]

Medications for irritability and its consequences include many classes of drugs. Randomized clinical trials support the use of citalopram[8] and sertraline[9] for irritability. The antimanic agent sodium valproate, which is widely used to reduce irritability and aggression in patients with dementia, has not been effective in randomized trials.[10] In a 16-week randomized, placebo-controlled trial for the treatment of agitation in patients with Alzheimer's disease, 34% of patients who received the high-potency typical antipsychotic drug haloperidol, trazodone or behavioral management, showed improvement. However, there was no significant difference between any of the active treatment groups and placebo[11] using the Cohen-Mansfield Agitation Inventory score[12] as the outcome measure. The atypical antipsychotic drugs risperidone, 1 mg/day,[13] and olanzapine, 5 mg/day,[14] appeared to be modestly effective on outcome measures such as the Behavioral Pathology in Alzheimer's Disease scale (BEHAVE-AD)[15] and the Neuropsychiatric Inventory[16] in patients with psychosis and behavioral disturbances associated with dementia.

Case reports suggest that sexual disinhibition, at least in men, is treatable with low-dose medroxyprogesterone.[17]

Psychotherapy

A very large number of behavioral and cognitive intervention techniques have been suggested for the reduction of behavioral

21

Highlights *in* treatment of behavioral symptoms in the dementias *2005–06*

WHAT'S IN?

- Viewing disturbed/disturbing behavior in context
- Objective scales for identifying and quantifying behavioral disturbance

WHAT'S OUT?

- Viewing any behavior that is disturbing to others as pathological
- Viewing disturbed behavior solely as a consequence of the patient's dementia
- Drug therapy without consideration of context

WHAT'S NEW?

- Black-box warning of adverse cardiovascular events for atypical antipsychotics in elderly people

WHAT'S NEEDED?

- Specific treatments for specific behaviors in specific contexts

disturbances in individuals with dementias,[18] but there are few randomized controlled trials other than the study cited above[11] and a trial that evaluated exercise plus behavioral management. The latter study reduced depressive symptoms and improved physical functioning, but demonstrated no significant impact on other behaviors.[19]

Treating the individual

There are few data on which to base treatment decisions for people with behavioral disturbances due to dementia. Behavioral symptoms in individuals with dementia tend to be evanescent and highly dependent on the interpersonal and environmental context. There are few specific treatments other than for depression.

The development of better treatment strategies depends on our willingness to see behavioral disturbances in dementia patients as the result of complex interactions that need to be understood on an individual basis. This individualized approach is likely to require a flexible combination of behavioral (including caregiver education), environmental and psychopharmacologic interventions. The clinician will need to be sensitive to the effects these approaches have on measures of patient and caregiver quality of life.

References

1. Weiner MF, Teri L. Psychological and behavioral management. In: Weiner MF, Lipton AM, eds. *The Dementias: Diagnosis, Treatment and Research*, 3rd edn. Washington, DC: American Psychiatric Publishing, 2003: 181–218.

2. Lyketsos CG, DelCampo L, Steinberg M et al. Treating depression in Alzheimer disease: efficacy and safety of sertraline therapy, and the benefits of depression reduction: the DIADS. *Arch Gen Psychiatry* 2003;60:737–46.

3. Sink KM, Holden KF, Yaffe K. Pharmacological treatment of neuropsychiatric symptoms of dementia: a review of the evidence. *JAMA* 2005;293:596–608.

4. Bullock R. Treatment of behavioural and psychiatric symptoms in dementia: implications of recent safety warnings. *Curr Med Res Opin* 2005;21:1–10.

5. McKeith I, Del Ser T, Spano P et al. Efficacy of rivastigmine in dementia with Lewy bodies: a randomised, double-blind, placebo-controlled international study. *Lancet* 2000;356:2031–6.

6. Fernandez HH, Wu CK, Ott BR. Pharmacotherapy of dementia with Lewy bodies. *Expert Opin Pharmacother* 2003;4:2027–37.

7. McCurry SM, Gibbons LE, Logsdon RG et al. Nighttime insomnia treatment and education for Alzheimer's disease: a randomized, controlled trial. *J Am Geriatr Soc* 2005;53:793–802.

8. Nyth AL, Gottfries CG. The clinical efficacy of citalopram in treatment of emotional disturbances in dementia disorders. A Nordic multicentre study. *Br J Psychiatry* 1990;157:894–901.

9. Lanctot KL, Herrmann N, van Reekum R et al. Gender, aggression and serotonergic function are associated with response to sertraline for behavioral disturbances in Alzheimer's disease. *Int J Geriatr Psychiatry* 2002;17:531–41.

10. Sival RC, Haffmans PM, Jansen PA et al. Sodium valproate in the treatment of aggressive behavior in patients with dementia – a randomized placebo controlled clinical trial. *Int J Geriatr Psychiatry* 2002;17:579–85.

11. Teri L, Logsdon RG, Peskind E et al. Treatment of agitation in AD: a randomized, placebo-controlled clinical trial. *Neurology* 2000;55: 1271–8.

12. Cohen-Mansfield J. Agitated behaviors in the elderly. II. Preliminary results in the cognitively deteriorated. *J Am Geriatr Soc* 1986;34:722–7.

13. Katz IR, Jeste DV, Mintzer JE et al. Comparison of risperidone and placebo for psychosis and behavioral disturbances associated with dementia: a randomized, double-blind trial. *J Clin Psychiatry* 1999;60:107–15.

14. Street JS, Clark WS, Gannon KS et al.; the HGEU Study Group. Olanzapine treatment of psychotic and behavioral symptoms in patients with Alzheimer disease in nursing care facilities: a double-blind, randomized, placebo-controlled trial. *Arch Gen Psychiatry* 2000;57: 968–76.

15. Reisberg B, Borenstein J, Salob SP et al. Behavioral symptoms in Alzheimer's disease: phenomenology and treatment. *J Clin Psychiatry* 1987;48(suppl):9–15.

16. Cummings JL, Mega M, Gray K et al. The Neuropsychiatric Inventory: comprehensive assessment of psychopathology in dementia. *Neurology* 1994;44:2308–14.

17. Weiner MF, Schneider LS. Drugs for behavioral, psychological, and cognitive symptoms. In: Weiner MF, Lipton AM, eds. *The Dementias: Diagnosis, Treatment and Research*, 3rd edn. Washington, DC: American Psychiatric Publishing, 2003: 219–84.

18. Volicer L, Hurley AC. Management of behavioral symptoms in progressive degenerative dementias. *J Gerontol A Biol Sci Med Sci* 2003;58:M837–45.

19. Teri L, Gibbons LE, McCurry SM et al. Exercise plus behavioral management in patients with Alzheimer disease: a randomized controlled trial. *JAMA* 2003;290: 2015–22.

Treatment of obsessive–compulsive disorder

Koen Schruers MD PhD
Research Institute of Brain and Behaviour, Maastricht University,
The Netherlands

Obsessive–compulsive disorder (OCD) is a severe anxiety disorder with a lifetime prevalence of 2–3%. It is characterized by obsessions, intrusive thoughts that evoke anxiety or discomfort, and compulsions – repetitive behavior aimed at reducing the discomfort and anxiety. Most patients develop the condition before the age of 35. Comorbidity with other psychiatric disorders is common, most often with depression.

Therapeutic possibilities have increased, so that prognosis has improved considerably in recent years. In spite of this progress, around 30% of patients with OCD remain relatively resistant to therapy.

Conventional therapeutic options are (cognitive) behavioral therapy, pharmacotherapy or a combination of both. When treatment resistance occurs, pharmacological augmentation strategies or neurosurgical interventions are available.

Cognitive behavioral therapy

Behavioral therapy in the form of exposure to the anxiety trigger and subsequent response prevention was the first empirically validated treatment for OCD. In this form of treatment, the patient is repeatedly exposed to their feared situation, but is not allowed to perform the rituals normally used to reduce the fear, until the fear subsides. While this form of therapy seems most effective in the hands of a therapist, there are indications that self-management interventions performed independently of the therapist could be effective as well.[1] Studies to evaluate brief interventions and computer-based interventions are scarce, small and short term, but do warrant further exploration. Future studies should also include measures of cost-effectiveness.[2]

Cognitive therapy for OCD focuses on the potential bias in reasoning displayed by the patients, in which they overestimate the level and likelihood of danger, and inflate the role of their own responsibility. Cognitive therapy is effective in the treatment of OCD, but does not seem more effective than the classic technique of exposure and response prevention.[1] However, a combination of cognitive therapy with elements of exposure has proven advantageous.[3] Recent evidence also suggests that cognitive behavioral group therapy might be an effective treatment option for OCD. However, the findings from this study need to be confirmed in a long-term, randomized, controlled trial.[4]

Pharmacotherapy

Serotonin-reuptake inhibitors (SRIs) have proven effective in the treatment of OCD, usually at high doses over long periods of time.[5] These drugs include tricyclic compounds such as clomipramine, but mostly selective SRIs (SSRIs) such as fluvoxamine, fluoxetine, paroxetine, sertraline and, more recently, citalopram. There are no large double-blind, randomized controlled studies that compare SRIs head to head. Meta-analyses suggest that all SSRIs have similar efficacy, but also that clomipramine is still more effective. Nevertheless, SSRIs are commonly preferred because of their more favorable side-effect profile.[1]

Drugs with little affinity for serotonin receptors such as desipramine appear to be less efficacious. On the other hand, the selective serotonin- and noradrenaline-reuptake inhibitor venlafaxine was recently shown to be effective.[6]

Pharmacotherapy and CBT

Few studies have directly compared cognitive behavioral therapy (CBT), pharmacotherapy and combination therapy. Those that have suggest that medication alone has less effect and is associated with higher relapse rates than CBT monotherapy or a combination of CBT and pharmacotherapy. However, the combination does not seem to be superior to CBT alone, at least in patients with uncomplicated OCD. In patients who present mainly with obsessions or with comorbid depression, combination therapy does appear to be more effective.[1]

Dealing with therapy resistance

The majority of patients with OCD can be effectively treated with CBT and conventional pharmacotherapy. However, a significant minority of around 30% fail to respond to these treatments. For these patients, several additional treatments have been proposed. Among these, augmentation of SRI treatment with a low dose of an antipsychotic is the best documented option. Studies have shown additional clinical improvement after augmentation with risperidone,[7] olanzapine[8] or quetiapine.[9] Of these, risperidone is the most documented.[7] In one study, haloperidol was shown only to have additional effect in a subset of patients with comorbid tic disorder.[10] Augmentation with different kinds of medications such as buspirone, lithium or thyroid hormone does not appear to have any additional value.[1]

Some open studies suggest that intravenous SRI administration with clomipramine or citalopram might be an option, but these findings need to be confirmed in controlled, double-blind studies.[5]

Some case studies mention the use of electroconvulsive therapy or repetitive transcranial magnetic stimulation (rTMS) as treatment for OCD. However, there is not sufficient evidence to promote the use of these techniques in OCD, even in treatment-resistant patients. It does seem, however, that rTMS might be useful as a tool to unravel the pathophysiology of OCD.[5]

Neurosurgery

The application of neurosurgical techniques in patients with treatment-refractory OCD has a long history. The most commonly used procedures are capsulotomy, cingulotomy, limbic leucotomy and subcaudate tractotomy (Table 1). Early reports were often overly optimistic about the effects and the potential side effects of these invasive procedures. Studies often did not include systematic

TABLE 1

Neurosurgical techniques for treatment-resistant OCD

Procedure	Description
Anterior capsulotomy	Production of small, bilateral lesions in the anterior limb of the internal capsule to interrupt frontothalamic pathways
Cingulotomy	Stereotactic placement of bilateral lesions in the anterior cingulate cortex
Limbic leucotomy	Production of three lesions in the lower medial quadrant of each frontal lobe and two lesions in each cingulum; in essence, this is a combination of a subcaudate tractotomy and a cingulotomy to disrupt multiple cortico–striato–thalamocortical interactions
Subcaudate tractotomy	Creation of a lesion to interrupt pathways between the orbitofrontal cortex and the thalamus
Deep-brain stimulation	Implantation of electrodes connected to a pacemaker to give continuous electric stimulation to the chosen area of the brain to interrupt the appropriate pathways; a reversible alternative to permanent lesion production

evaluation of personality changes or neuropsychological dysfunction. Furthermore, one must keep in mind that any surgical intervention is associated with the risk of bleeding or infection.

The reported success rates in early studies vary between 50% and 67%. However, recent long-term, follow-up studies have shown that rates around 30% are probably more accurate.[11] Another drawback of these lesion studies, for obvious ethical reasons, is the lack of a control condition. Use of the so-called gamma knife could overcome this problem, but to date no such studies using this technique have been published.

Highlights in **treatment of obsessive–compulsive disorder** *2005–06*

WHAT'S IN?

- Deep-brain stimulation for treatment-resistant obsessive–compulsive disorder (OCD)
- Treatment based on insight into the pathophysiology of the condition
- Intensive behavioral therapy programs
- Computer-based cognitive behavioral interventions

WHAT'S OUT?

- Lesion neurosurgery for treatment-resistant OCD
- Electroconvulsive therapy for OCD

Chronic deep-brain stimulation (DBS) is a new neurosurgical technique, originally developed for patients with treatment-resistant Parkinson's disease. Instead of making a lesion, an electrode is placed in the brain and connected to a pacemaker. Continuous electric stimulation appears to have the same effect as other procedures that would create a lesion instead. That this novel technique is completely reversible is a major advantage, particularly in patients who experience intolerable side effects. The procedure therefore only presents the general surgical risk of bleeding or infection.[1] Furthermore, DBS allows the introduction of a control condition. Preliminary data on the efficacy of this procedure show a beneficial effect in patients with treatment-resistant OCD.[12] It seems that DBS might be a less invasive but equally effective treatment option to the more common surgical procedures for this disabling condition.[13] The results need to be confirmed in larger, double-blind, controlled studies.

References

1. Schruers K, Koning K, Luermans J et al. Obsessive–compulsive disorder: a critical review of therapeutic perspectives. *Acta Psychiatr Scand* 2005;111:261–71.

2. Barlow JH, Ellard DR, Hainsworth JM et al. A review of self-management interventions for panic disorders, phobias and obsessive–compulsive disorders. *Acta Psychiatr Scand* 2005;111:272–85.

3. Fisher PL, Wells A. Experimental modification of beliefs in obsessive–compulsive disorder: a test of the metacognitive model. *Behav Res Ther* 2005;43:821–9.

4. Braga DT, Cordioli AV, Niederauer K, Manfro GG. Cognitive-behavioral group therapy for obsessive–compulsive disorder: a 1-year follow-up. *Acta Psychiatr Scand* 2005;112:180–6.

5. Pallanti S, Hollander E, Goodman WK. A qualitative analysis of nonresponse: management of treatment-refractory obsessive–compulsive disorder. *J Clin Psychiatry* 2004;65(suppl 14):6–10.

6. Denys D, van Megen HJ, van der Wee N, Westenberg HG. A double-blind switch study of paroxetine and venlafaxine in obsessive–compulsive disorder. *J Clin Psychiatry* 2004; 65:37–43.

7. Li X, May RS, Tolbert LC et al. Risperidone and haloperidol augmentation of serotonin reuptake inhibitors in refractory obsessive–compulsive disorder: a crossover study. *J Clin Psychiatry* 2005;66: 736–43.

8. Shapira NA, Ward HE, Mandoki M et al. A double-blind placebo-controlled trial of olanzapine addition in fluoxetine-refractory obsessive–compulsive disorder. *Biol Psychiatry* 2004;55:553–5.

9. Denys D, de Geus F, van Megen HJ, Westenberg HG. A double-blind, randomized, placebo-controlled trial of quetiapine addition in patients with obsessive–compulsive disorder refractory to serotonin reuptake inhibitors. *J Clin Psychiatry* 2004;65: 1040–8.

10. McDougle CJ, Goodman WK, Leckman JF et al. Haloperidol addition in fluvoxamine-refractory obsessive–compulsive disorder. A double-blind, placebo-controlled study in patients with and without tics. *Arch Gen Psychiatry* 1994;51: 302–8.

11. Dougherty DD, Baer L, Cosgrove GR et al. Prospective long-term follow-up of 44 patients who received cingulotomy for treatment-refractory obsessive–compulsive disorder. *Am J Psychiatry* 2002;159: 269–75.

12. Nuttin B, Cosyns P, Demeulemeester H et al. Electrical stimulation in anterior limbs of internal capsules in patients with obsessive–compulsive disorder. *Lancet* 1999;354:1526.

13. Gabriels L, Cosyns P, Nuttin B et al. Deep brain stimulation for treatment-refractory obsessive–compulsive disorder: psycho-pathological and neuropsychological outcome in three cases. *Acta Psychiatr Scand* 2003;107:275–82.

Hoarding

Thomas Maier MD

Psychiatric Department, Zurich University Hospital, Switzerland

'Hoarding', as a term in scientific literature, refers to the storing of food as a natural behavior in certain species of animals. In psychiatry, the term is now used to specify behavioral abnormalities characterized by the excessive collection and accumulation of objects of little or no use. This type of behavior is mainly observed in association with obsessive–compulsive disorder (OCD) and in geriatric populations. In spite of the growing body of literature on hoarding, its psychopathological status remains controversial.[1,2]

In view of the fact that there is no consistent definition, it is questionable whether 'hoarding', without further specification, is a meaningful term within psychiatric literature. In fact, hoarding in humans is a complex and variable behavioral phenomenon associated with a broad spectrum of mental disorders. Severe self-neglect is a possible, but not inevitable, consequence of hoarding. The behavior is observed even in the absence of diagnosable mental disorders, so it is not a priori pathological. The psychopathological structure of hoarding is variously composed of elements of OCD, impulse-control deficits and stereotypic tic-like behavior.[3,4]

Possible link with obsessive–compulsive disorder

Over the past decade, the association of hoarding with OCD has been the intense focus of research. Hoarding is assessed by standard OCD screening instruments such as the Yale–Brown Obsessive–Compulsive Scale (Y–BOCS),[5] and several authors have attempted to identify a hoarding subgroup within the OCD population.

The results of these studies suggest a distinct placement for hoarding within the spectrum of OCD.[6–10] Hoarding is more time-stable than most other OCD symptoms, but it is associated with less insight, is often ego-syntonic and shows poorer treatment response. Frost et al. found hoarding obsessions in one-third of patients with OCD and hoarding compulsions in a quarter of them.[11] Compared with OCD non-hoarders, OCD hoarders showed higher levels of general psychopathology: they had higher scores of depression, anxiety, family and social disability, and personality disorders. However, Grisham et al. concluded that these findings applied only to hoarders with additional OCD symptoms and not to 'pure' hoarders.[1] Saxena et al. even introduced the notion of 'compulsive hoarding syndrome', and presented neurobiological findings to support the idea of a distinct hoarding subgroup or variant of OCD.[12]

Although not mentioned as a symptom of OCD in the fourth edition of the *Diagnostic and Statistical Manual of Mental Disorders* (DSM-IV), hoarding is considered by most researchers to be a regular symptom of OCD.[3,6,7,10,12] However, this opinion remains controversial and was explicitly rejected in two recent studies.[1,2] Wu and Watson concluded in their meticulous study that there was no empirical evidence to identify hoarding as a symptom of OCD.[2] In accord with Grisham's findings,[1] they demonstrated that hoarding correlates no better with a diagnosis of OCD than other non-OCD symptoms such as depression or anxiety, and they proposed that hoarding be omitted as a specific symptom of OCD.

These marked differences in appraisal may partly result from imprecise concepts of hoarding. In many studies, there is no clear differentiation between hoarding 'obsessions', 'compulsions' and 'behavior', and often it remains unclear which of these elements of hoarding has been assessed. For example, OCD hoarders usually do not compulsively collect items, making the notion of 'compulsive hoarding' misleading. Instead, they fail to discard common everyday objects due to obsessive thoughts.[1,13] Indeed, the core feature of hoarding in OCD is an avoiding behavior, not a compulsion. When the behavioral abnormality actually consists of excessive collectionism, there is usually more overlap with impulse-control disorders.[1,2,14]

In the elderly

The issue of hoarding is widely discussed in the literature on geriatrics, for the most part independently of the literature on OCD. A lot of attention is paid to subsequent nursing problems and public health issues associated with hoarding.[15]

Hoarding of large quantities of rubbish, severe self-neglect, social retreat, lack of insight and refusal of treatment have been described in elderly subjects since the mid-1970s.[16] The term Diogenes syndrome has been used to describe cases characterized by extreme self-neglect, the hoarding of rubbish and living in general squalor,[17,18] although it is now a term avoided by most authors. Owing to the obvious split between research on OCD and geriatrics, it is unclear if self-neglecting elderly people and OCD hoarders overlap to some extent.

In a sample of 233 adults who had refused the assistance of community service providers (e.g. meals-on-wheels, home helps, house cleaning etc.), Hurley et al. found 54% with hoarding behavior.[19] However, these researchers found a history of psychiatric illness (mostly alcohol or drug abuse) in only 37% of the total sample, and they did not report any cases of OCD. In a similar large community study of people living in squalor, Halliday et al. found hoarding behavior in 51% of the neglected households.[20] Even though the authors diagnosed mental disorders in 70% of the subjects, they too did not report a single case of OCD. In both studies, hoarding behavior was not described in detail, but defined by the result, that is, the accumulation of items of little or no use in the dwelling.

In a sample of 133 dementia patients, Hwang et al. found 23% with hoarding behavior.[21] The detailed description of the observed behavior in these patients suggests a mainly repetitive motor action like grasping and reaching for objects. These actions are performed without deliberate intention and are associated with similar symptoms such as hyperphagia and pilfering. Some authors consider hoarding to be a common symptom of dementia,[22,23] although the exact nature of hoarding behavior in these patients has not been specified.

Highlights in **hoarding** 2005–06

WHAT'S IN?

- Acceptance of hoarding as a generic term for a multifaceted behavioral phenomenon

- An awareness that hoarding behavior in humans can variously be composed of obsessive–compulsive symptoms, impulse-control deficits and stereotypic tic-like motor activity

- An individualized approach to the assessment of hoarding behavior, so that the appropriate treatment can be adapted to the underlying disorder

WHAT'S OUT?

- Hoarding as a defined symptom
- Hoarding as a defined syndrome
- Use of the term hoarding without further specification

In association with other disorders

A confusing variety of other studies have been published on hoarding or hoarding-like behaviors in association with different mental or physical disorders such as anorexia nervosa, attention deficit hyperactivity disorder (ADHD), chronic schizophrenia, Tourette syndrome, Prader–Willi syndrome and brain damage etc.[4] When analyzing these disparate papers, it becomes apparent that the term 'hoarding' is used to label a variety of different behavioral phenomena. Hoarding in patients with residual schizophrenia, brain damage, mental retardation or tic disorders is mostly characterized by stereotypic tic-like motor activity without aim and intention. Unlike OCD hoarders, these patients have no obsessional thoughts or anxiety about discarding their hoarded items.

An interesting and maybe integrative perspective is presented in a recent paper by Anderson et al.[24] They report neuroanatomic findings in 86 patients who developed pathological collecting behavior after brain damage. These patients had cerebral lesions in the mesial frontal regions (including the anterior gyrus cinguli) of the brain, which is consistent with Saxena's findings of neurobiological abnormalities in OCD hoarders.[12]

Finally, there is a large body of self-help literature about partly non-clinical hoarders (self-named 'pack rats' or 'messies'). Some of them are organized in self-help groups and seem to have fair social functioning. There may be subjects with OCD or impulse-control disorders among them, but there are no epidemiological data available on these populations.

References

1. Grisham JR, Brown TA, Liverant GI, Campbell-Sills L. The distinctiveness of compulsive hoarding from obsessive–compulsive disorder. *J Anxiety Disord* 2005;19: 767–79.

2. Wu KD, Watson D. Hoarding and its relation to obsessive–compulsive disorder. *Behav Res Ther* 2005;43: 897–921.

3. Steketee G, Frost R. Compulsive hoarding: current status of the research. *Clin Psychol Rev* 2003;23: 905–27.

4. Maier T. On phenomenology and classification of hoarding: a review. *Acta Psychiatr Scand* 2004;110: 323–37.

5. Foa EB, Huppert JD, Leiberg S et al. The Obsessive–Compulsive Inventory: development and validation of a short version. *Psychol Assess* 2002;14:485–96.

6. Samuels J, Bienvenu OJ 3rd, Riddle MA et al. Hoarding in obsessive–compulsive disorder: results from a case-control study. *Behav Res Ther* 2002;40:517–28.

7. Mataix-Cols D, Rosario-Campos MC, Leckman JF. A multidimensional model of obsessive–compulsive disorder. *Am J Psychiatry* 2005;162: 228–38.

8. Saxena S, Maidment KM, Vapnik T et al. Obsessive–compulsive hoarding: symptom severity and response to multimodal treatment. *J Clin Psychiatry* 2002;63:21–7.

9. Mataix-Cols D, Rauch SL, Manzo PA et al. Use of factor-analyzed symptom dimensions to predict outcome with serotonin reuptake inhibitors and placebo in the treatment of obsessive–compulsive disorder. *Am J Psychiatry* 1999;156:1409–16.

10. Rufer M, Grothusen A, Mass R et al. Temporal stability of symptom dimensions in adult patients with obsessive–compulsive disorder. *J Affect Disord* 2005;88:99–102.

11. Frost RO, Steketee G, Williams LF, Warren R. Mood, personality disorder symptoms and disability in obsessive–compulsive hoarders: a comparison with clinical and nonclinical controls. *Behav Res Ther* 2000;38:1071–81.

12. Saxena S, Brody AL, Maidment KM et al. Cerebral glucose metabolism in obsessive–compulsive hoarding. *Am J Psychiatry* 2004; 161:1038–48.

13. Amdur MA. Comment on hoarding. *Am J Psychiatry* 2005;162:1031.

14. Frost RO, Steketee G, Williams L. Compulsive buying, compulsive hoarding, and obsessive–compulsive disorder. *Behav Ther* 2002,33:201–14.

15. Lauder W, Anderson I, Barclay A. A framework for good practice in interagency interventions with cases of self-neglect. *J Psychiatr Ment Health Nurs* 2005;12:192–8.

16. Clark AN, Mankikar GD, Gray I. Diogenes syndrome. A clinical study of gross neglect in old age. *Lancet* 1975;1:366–8.

17. Reyes-Ortiz CA. Diogenes syndrome: the self-neglect elderly. *Compr Ther* 2001;27:117–21.

18. Montero-Odasso M, Schapira M, Duque G et al. Is collectionism a diagnostic clue for Diogenes syndrome? *Int J Geriatr Psychiatry* 2005;20:709–11.

19. Hurley M, Scallan E, Johnson H, De La Harpe D. Adult service refusers in the greater Dublin area. *Ir Med J* 2000;93:208–11.

20. Halliday G, Banerjee S, Philpot M, Macdonald A. Community study of people who live in squalor. *Lancet* 2000;355:882–6.

21. Hwang JP, Tsai SJ, Yang CH et al. Hoarding behavior in dementia. A preliminary report. *Am J Geriatr Psychiatry* 1998;6:285–9.

22. Hwang JP, Yang CH, Tsai SJ, Liu KM. Behavioural disturbances in psychiatric inpatients with dementia of the Alzheimer's type in Taiwan. *Int J Geriatr Psychiatry* 1997;12:902–6.

23. Stein DJ, Laszlo B, Marais E et al. Hoarding symptoms in patients on a geriatric psychiatry inpatient unit. *S Afr Med J* 1997;87:1138–40.

24. Anderson SW, Damasio H, Damasio AR. A neural basis for collecting behaviour in humans. *Brain* 2005;128:201–12.

Psychotherapies in treatment-resistant depression

Susan McPherson BSc MSc

Tavistock & Portman NHS Trust, London, UK/University of Essex, UK

Treatment-resistant depression has been defined as major depression with failure to respond to two adequate trials of medication with different classes of antidepressant.[1,2] Because consensus on this precise definition has emerged only recently, it has not been employed in many completed trials of psychotherapy for treatment-resistant depression. However, the studies discussed below have all specified major depression with at least one failure of antidepressant medication.

Although treatment-resistant depression is commonly a chronic condition, chronic depression is not necessarily treatment resistant. This distinction is particularly important when assessing the effectiveness of treatments. Studies that only specify chronicity without referring to the failure of antidepressant medication are not discussed here.

So far, data from controlled, psychotherapy evaluation studies have been reported on:
- cognitive behavioral therapy (CBT)
- cognitive therapy (CT)
- cognitive group therapy (CGT).

Each of these psychotherapies is defined in Table 1.

Cognitive behavioral therapy

Two controlled trials of this type of psychotherapy have been reported. The first found 26–36 weeks of CBT to be significantly more effective ($p < 0.05$) than no treatment, as observed in a waiting-list group.[3] The second demonstrated that 15 sessions of inpatient CBT was as effective as antidepressant medication.[4] Although both promising, the average treatment duration in the first

TABLE 1

Definition of psychotherapeutic approaches

Cognitive behavioral therapy
- Identifies distorted or dysfunctional thoughts and behavior patterns, which influence a person's mood or behavior
- Behavioral therapy aims to weaken the connections between difficult situations and habitual reactions to them
- Cognitive therapy (see below)

Cognitive therapy
- Replaces inaccurate or distorted thoughts/perceptions with more rational, adaptive thoughts/beliefs
- Focuses on more positive ways of thinking about, and coping with, life events and relationships

Cognitive group therapy
- Facilitates interaction and vicarious learning by watching others solve similar problems
- Provides the opportunity for patients to learn more about themselves and their effect on others through feedback from others in the group

trial was more than twice that in the second study and much more lengthy than standard CBT (usually 10–15 sessions). Therefore, it is not possible to infer that standard, brief CBT would be effective for this group. Rather, to be effective CBT must be fairly lengthy or provided with added inpatient support.

The duration of treatment in trials is a particularly important factor to take into account when assessing the effectiveness of treatment. It needs to be similar enough to the duration of treatment employed in standard clinical practice to have clinical relevance, and must be cost-effective as well as clinically effective.

No follow-up data or information on changes in quality of life were published from either of these studies. Such data are of significant import for informing clinical practice given the chronic, disabling nature of treatment-resistant depression and the significant disease burden it represents.[5] Nevertheless, CBT may be as effective as antidepressant medication and may be a preferable treatment option for patients, given that there were no dropouts from the CBT groups in either study and an attrition rate of 20% in the medicated group in the second study.

Cognitive therapy

One controlled study has been reported in which 15–30 outpatient sessions of CT were found to be significantly more effective than antidepressant medication ($p < 0.01$).[6] This is a particularly promising result, given that the range of 15–30 sessions provided in this study approached that used in standard practice, unlike the first CBT study described above. However, the attrition rate for the CT group was 43%, which is very high, suggesting that CT may only suit some patients. Further studies are needed to identify factors likely to lead to drop out. This study also lacked any reporting of follow-up data or quality-of-life indicators, which, as discussed, are essential in the assessment of treatment-resistant depression.

A second study found 22 weeks of CT to be as effective as social skills training, although both groups improved (overall $p < 0.05$).[7] Both groups also received inpatient care and antidepressant medication. No follow-up results or data on quality of life were published. This study is difficult to interpret given that there was no genuine control group, and any effects of psychotherapy cannot be disentangled from the effects of inpatient care including medication. Such studies emphasize the importance of adequate control groups in future research.

Cognitive group therapy

One controlled trial compared the response of patients who received 16–20 sessions of CGT with those who used a self-help manual.[8] Both groups improved and no patients dropped out, but there was no significant difference between the groups and no data on quality of life were reported. Although follow-up scores at 6 and 12 months indicated that the improvement was maintained, no significance level was reported. This is again a promising finding, but the importance of reporting statistical and clinical significance cannot be overstated. Furthermore, improvements in the self-help group serve as an important reminder that an intended control group can turn out to be a comparative treatment. In this instance, the study was left without an adequate control group and therefore provided insufficient evidence from which to draw firm conclusions, other than that CGT may be as effective as other simple psychological management strategies such as self-help.

Better study design and follow-up data needed

The published literature to date is particularly poor in terms of the quantity and quality of study design and data reporting. It is therefore particularly difficult to draw any firm conclusions about any of the treatments described here or to make recommendations for practice. At present, the body of literature in this area is such that it is only possible to make recommendations for further research and for this research to be granted adequate funding.

None of the controlled studies of psychotherapy for treatment-resistant depression report significance levels for long-term outcomes or improvements in quality of life, which are of vital importance in this patient group. Furthermore, the lack of adequate control groups in the studies to date suggests that researchers in this field continue to struggle to find an appropriate control group that is ethically comfortable for providers of psychological care whilst satisfying good research design principles. In the absence of an absolute efficacy study establishing a basal rate of effectiveness of any treatment, then relative efficacy studies with null findings (i.e. both treatments 'improve' the patient to approximately the same degree) are uninterpretable. Both treatments may have been equally effective, equally ineffective (relative to spontaneous variations in the condition), or equally harmful in hindering the short-term improvements that may have occurred without treatment and thus lowering the slope of recovery. This applies just as much to social skills training as to self-help.

Highlights in psychotherapies in treatment-resistant depression 2005–06

WHAT'S IN?

- Cognitive behavioral therapy (CBT), which may be as effective as antidepressant medication if provided for sufficient duration or with additional inpatient care, and may be more acceptable to patients

- Cognitive therapy (CT), which may be more effective than antidepressant medication, but less acceptable to some patients

- Cognitive group therapy (CGT), as it may be helpful and acceptable to patients, although it is not yet clear whether it is any more helpful than antidepressant medication or treatment as usual

WHAT'S OUT?

- Cognitive group therapy if it turns out to be no more effective than simple psychological management techniques such as self-help

WHAT'S NEEDED?

- Adequately controlled trials of CBT, CT, CGT, psychoeducational group therapy and psychodynamic psychotherapy, with long-term follow-up data and inclusion of a range of quality-of-life and other non-symptom outcomes

- Studies that clearly define the method by which treatment resistance was established

- Studies with greater power, stronger methods of analysis and better data reporting

Treatment-as-usual control groups are recommended for future trials in this area and randomization is also suggested as an important design feature. Trials of other forms of psychotherapy are also needed, including psychodynamic psychotherapy and psychoeducational group therapy (which has already shown some promising results on long-term follow-up and quality-of-life outcomes in uncontrolled studies).[9]

References

1. Souery D, Amsterdam J, de Montigny C et al. Treatment resistant depression: methodological overview and operational criteria. *Eur Neuropsychopharmacol* 1999;9: 83–91.

2. Sackeim H. The definition and meaning of treatment-resistant depression. *J Clin Psychiatry* 2001;62(suppl 16):10–17.

3. Harpin RE, Liberman RP, Marks I et al. Cognitive-behavior therapy for chronically depressed patients. A controlled pilot study. *J Nerv Ment Dis* 1982;170:295–301.

4. Barker WA, Scott J, Eccleston D. The Newcastle chronic depression study: results of a treatment regime. *Int Clin Psychopharmacol* 1987;2: 261–72.

5. Greden JF. The burden of disease for treatment-resistant depression. *J Clin Psychiatry* 2001;62(suppl 16): 26–31.

6. Moore RG, Blackburn IM. Cognitive therapy in the treatment of non-responders to antidepressant medication: a controlled pilot study. *Behav Cogn Psychother* 1997;25: 251–9.

7. Miller IW, Bishop SB, Norman WH, Keitner GI. Cognitive/behavioral therapy and pharmacotherapy with chronic, drug-refractory depressed inpatients: a note of optimism. *Behav Psychother* 1985;13:320–7.

8. Bristow M, Bright J. Group cognitive therapy in chronic depression: results from two intervention studies. *Behav Cogn Psychother* 1995;23:373–80.

9. Swan J, Sorrell E, MacVicar B et al. "Coping with depression": an open study of the efficacy of a group psychoeducational intervention in chronic, treatment-refractory depression. *J Affect Disord* 2004;82: 125–9.

Suicide in China

Zhang Jie PhD
SUNY College at Buffalo, New York, USA

The study of suicide in China is relatively new, but over the past
2 decades the number of studies has risen each year.[1] However, most
of the studies have been published in Chinese journals, and have
provided only limited and regional data; only a few have appeared in
English-language journals. Because of the relatively short history of
Chinese suicidology, few data have been available for longitudinal
studies.

Epidemiology

In China, the official suicide rate is 22.2 per 100 000 people,[2]
although estimates vary. For example, a World Mental Health Report
in 1995 put the overall suicide rate in China at 17.1,[3] a study by
Phillips and Liu reported a rate as high as 28.7,[4] while research
conducted at the Harvard School of Public Health reported a rate of
30.3.[5] The most recent study by Phillips et al. reported a mean annual
suicide rate of 23 per 100 000 and a total of 287 000 deaths due
to suicide per year. These last researchers concluded that suicide
accounts for 3.6% of all deaths in China and is the fifth most
important cause of death in the country.[6] Figure 1, which summarizes
the Chinese suicide rate by gender, age and location, is derived from
World Health Organization (WHO) data from 1987–1994.[7,8]

Suicide is the leading cause of death among 15–34 year-olds,
accounting for 19% of all deaths in this age group. The number of
suicides committed by women is 25% higher than that by men.
Figures from rural areas are three times higher than those in urban
areas for both men and women, across all age groups and over
time.[6] The enormous toll of suicide in China constitutes both an
urgent public health problem and an unmatched opportunity for
research.

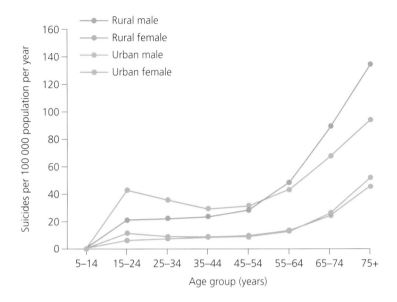

Figure 1: Chinese suicide rates (averaged for 1987–1994) by age, gender and location. Adapted from World Health Organization data.

Risk factors

Although suicide rates are higher for women in China than in the West, known risk factors are very similar between countries. Studies have indicated a number of factors that confer risk in China as well as in Western industrialized nations.[9–18] These include:

- psychiatric illness
- a prior history of suicide attempts
- acute and chronic stressors
- interpersonal conflict.

Social and cultural factors no doubt account for the difference in suicide rates between countries, yet these factors have gone unmeasured, which has significantly limited the research on suicide prevention.

Each country, and even each region within a country, has characteristic social values and norms generally held by its people.

45

The social values and cultural issues associated with suicide in China will differ in many respects from those that influence suicide rates in, for example, the USA. Furthermore, China is a developing society, and some of the social factors associated with suicide may be very different in another decade. Nonetheless, by demonstrating the association of such factors with suicide risk in China, we will learn critical lessons about the role of cultural factors in general, and provide a model for future work in this important area.

Higher suicide rate in women. Worldwide, the suicide rate in men is generally three times that in women.[19,20] In the USA, for example, men of all racial categories account for about 78.8% of all suicides each year.[21] Uniquely, in China, women who commit suicide outnumber men who do so by 25%.[22]

The Global Burden of Disease study found that China accounts for 56.6% of all suicides by women worldwide. This is an astonishing figure considering that only 21% of the world's female population lives in China. The study also found that the rate of suicide among Chinese women is nearly five times the world average.[23] This inverse gender ratio is speculated to be a function of Chinese culture.

Inverse gender ratio. As discussed above, China is the only known country where a greater percentage of women than men commit suicide.[24] However, the male/female ratios of completed suicides in Asian societies in general, are lower than those in the West: Hong Kong (1.1), Singapore (1.3), Japan (1.8), Taiwan (1.5), India (1.4), Philippines (1.5), South Korea (2.2).[25–27]

The inverse ratio in China may reflect China-specific factors of Asian culture. Dr Arthur Kleinman of Harvard University noted that Asian societies with low male/female ratios are generally found in areas dominated by Confucian ethics (personal communication, 2002). China may also differ from other Asian cultures in its communist ideology, which has been reinforced among the population since 1949.

Highlights *in* **suicide in China** *2005–06*

WHAT'S IN?

- Statistics that demonstrate unique gender ratios in Chinese suicide rates
- Research on the effects of pesticides used in rural areas on the female suicide rate in China
- Psychological autopsy methods to study suicide in China
- An awareness of the psychiatric disorders that influence the Chinese suicide rate

WHAT'S NEEDED?

- More rigorous research with more sophisticated methodology
- Re-evaluation of the effects of mental disorders on Chinese suicide
- Focus on the cultural factors that may be associated with the unique gender ratios
- Study of Chinese suicide in a global context

As well as questioning why women are at higher risk of suicide than men, we should also ask why Chinese men are less likely to kill themselves. In modern China, the communist ideology on gender egalitarianism clashes with traditional Confucian sexism, and the conflict between the positive expectation of the female role in society and the rural reality has increased the psychological strain on Chinese women.

Researchers have suggested a number of reasons for this unique gender ratio in Chinese suicide, including easy accessibility to lethal but less violent suicide methods such as pesticides (which are generally found to be more appealing methods of suicide to women), as well as less accessible emergency care in the countryside (to which women have especially limited access as they tend to be poorer) and the relative deprivation in rural China.[8,28,29] However, in urban China, where these three conditions do not prevail, there are still higher suicide rates in women than in men.

To better understand the inverse gender ratio and to develop better suicide prevention measures, we need to study the effect of the prevailing culture on suicidal behaviors. Confucian ethics and communist ideology may have resulted in strain or frustration in certain young minds in a developing country. For example, the discrepancy between deep-rooted Confucian values of inequality between the sexes and enforced communist equalitarianism ideology may result in social pressure and individual frustration among young Chinese women.

References

1. Zhang J, Jia S, Wieczorek WF et al. An overview of suicide research in China. *Arch Suicide Res* 2002;6:167–84.

2. Yin D. Current status of mental health work in China: problems and recommendations. *Chin Ment Health J* 2002;14:4–5 (in Chinese).

3. Murray CJL, Lopez AD. Global Health Statistics: A Compendium of Incidence, Prevalence, and Mortality Estimates for Over 200 Conditions. Boston, MA: Harvard University Press, 1996.

4. Phillips MR, Liu H. Suicide in China: an overview. Paper presented at the Befrienders Conference, Kuala Lumpur, Malaysia, 1996.

5. Murray CJL, Lopez AD. The Global Burden of Disease. Geneva, Switzerland: World Health Organization, Harvard School of Public Health, World Bank, 1996.

6. Phillips MR, Li X, Zhang Y. Suicide rates in China, 1995–99. *Lancet* 2002;359:835–40.

7. Yang GH, Zhou LN, Huang ZJ, Chen AP. The trend and geographic distribution of suicide in Chinese population. *Zhonghua Liu Xing Bing Xue Za Zhi* 2004;25:280–4 (in Chinese).

8. Zhang J. Understanding Chinese suicide with a comparison of national data. *Am Rev China Stud* 2000;1: 9–29.

9. Bertolote JM, Fleischmann A, De Leo D et al. Suicide attempts, plans, and ideation in culturally diverse sites: the WHO SUPRE-MISS community survey. *Psychol Med* 2005;35:1457–65.

10. Chiu HF, Yip PS, Chi I et al. Elderly suicide in Hong Kong – a case-controlled psychological autopsy study. *Acta Psychiatr Scand* 2004; 109:299–305.

11. Ho TP, Tay MS. Suicides in general hospitals in Hong Kong: retrospective study. *Hong Kong Med J* 2004;10:319–24.

12. Liu X, Tein JY. Life events, psychopathology, and suicidal behavior in Chinese adolescents. *J Affect Disord* 2005;86:195–203.

13. Phillips MR, Yang G, Li S, Li Y. Suicide and the unique prevalence pattern of schizophrenia in mainland China: a retrospective observational study. *Lancet* 2004;364:1062–8.

14. Ran MS, Wu QH, Conwell Y et al. Suicidal behavior among inpatients with schizophrenia and mood disorders in Chengdu, China. *Suicide Life Threat Behav* 2004; 34:311–9.

15. Shen Y, Li H, Gu N et al. Relationship between suicidal behavior of psychotic inpatients and serotonin transporter gene in Han Chinese. *Neuroscience Lett* 2004;372:94–8.

16. Tsoh J, Chiu HF, Duberstein PR et al. Attempted suicide in elderly Chinese persons: a multi-group, controlled study. *Am J Geriatr Psychiatry* 2005;13:562–71.

17. Zhang J, Conwell Y, Zhou L, Jiang C. Culture, risk factors and suicide in rural China: a psychological autopsy case control study. *Acta Psychiatr Scand* 2004;110:430–7.

18. IOM (Institute of Medicine). Reducing suicide: a national imperative. Washington, DC: National Academy Press, 2002.

19. Brockington L. Suicide in women. *Int Clin Psychopharmacol* 2001;16(suppl 2):S7–19.

20. Pritchard C. Suicide in the People's Republic of China categorized by age and gender: evidence of the influence of culture on suicide. *Acta Psychiatr Scand* 1996;93:362–7.

21. Maris RW. Suicide. In: Borgatta EF, Borgatta ML, eds. *Encyclopedia of Sociology*, vol 4. New York: Macmillan, 1992.

22. Qin P, Mortensen PB. Specific characteristics of suicide in China. *Acta Psychiatr Scand* 2001;103: 117–21.

23. Macleod L. The dying fields. *Far East Econ Rev* 1998;23:62–3.

24. WHO (World Health Organization). *Mental Health and Brain Disorders: Suicide Rates (per 100,000)*. Geneva: World Health Organization, 2001. www.who.int/mental_health/prevention/suicide_rates/en/index.html [accessed February 10, 2006].

25. Canetto SS, Sakinofsky I. The gender paradox in suicide. *Suicide Life Threat Behav* 1998;28:1–23.

26. Taiwan Government, 2003. www.stat.gov.tw/bs2/2002Year Book.pdf

27. WHO (World Health Organization). The World Health Report 1999 – making a difference. Geneva, Switzerland: WHO, 1999. www.who.int/whr/1999/en/whr99_en.pdf

28. Li ZJ, Chen SY, Zhou J, Wu YQ. The study of poisoning-suicide-attempted patients in emergency departments of 25 hospitals in China. *Zhonghua Liu Xing Bing Xue Za Zhi* 2004;25:285–7 (in Chinese).

29. Phillips MR, Yang G, Zhang Y et al. Risk factors for suicide in China: a national case-control psychological autopsy study. *Lancet* 2002;360:1728–36.

The physical health of people with schizophrenia

Robin McCreadie DSc MD FRCPsych

Department of Clinical Research, Crichton Royal Hospital, Dumfries, UK

It has long been known that people with schizophrenia, both men and women, die at an earlier age – on average 10 years younger – than other members of the general population. Suicide is the most notable cause, but this is now believed to account for only about 5% of deaths.[1] Natural causes predominate, with more deaths due to gastrointestinal, cardiovascular and respiratory disease (but possibly not cancer)[2] than in the general population. Other conditions that are more common in people with schizophrenia include eye cataracts and diabetes; there has also been much recent interest in the metabolic syndrome (a group of metabolic risk factors, including abdominal obesity, dyslipidemia, hypertension and high levels of fasting glucose). Dental health also tends to be poorer.[3]

Factors affecting physical health

There are three main putative etiologic factors that contribute to the poor physical health of individuals with schizophrenia:

- the illness itself
- lifestyle
- medication.

The illness itself. Two recent studies from Dublin found that drug-naïve, first-episode patients had greater visceral obesity[4] and impaired fasting glucose levels[5] than healthy volunteers. People with schizophrenia were also more insulin resistant, and had higher levels of insulin and cortisol. The principal author of these studies suggested that the findings may be related to a subtle disturbance of the hypothalamic–pituitary–adrenal axis, which in turn may be an inherent part of the condition.

Lifestyle. The lifestyle of many people with schizophrenia is poor, especially those who have been ill for many years (Table 1). They are known to eat poorly and smoke heavily, the two most important causes of cardiovascular disease. In addition, most people with schizophrenia are overweight or obese.

Smoking. The majority of individuals with schizophrenia smoke, men more so than women (70% vs 40%), while nearly two-thirds (65%) are heavy smokers, that is, they smoke more than 25 cigarettes per day.[6] It is not clear why this is the case. Most people with schizophrenia start smoking before first presentation of the illness, so it is not the florid illness per se that makes them start. Fewer give up smoking compared with the general population. They may continue to smoke to ameliorate their symptoms, or the dopamine blockade produced by antipsychotic medication may lead them to smoke more heavily to produce the 'reward' effect. Whatever the reason, their smoking habits undoubtedly contribute to the excess number of deaths due to respiratory disease.

Poor dietary habits. It is now well recognized that the dietary habits of people with schizophrenia are poor.[7] Compared with the general population, fewer individuals with schizophrenia consume acceptable quantities of fruit, vegetables, milk, potatoes and pulses. The recommended daily intake of fruit and vegetables (an important source of micronutrients) is five portions; research has shown that people with schizophrenia consume only 16 portions per week.

TABLE 1

Lifestyle issues in people with schizophrenia

- Cigarette smoking (often heavy)
- Poor dietary habits (especially a low intake of fruit and vegetables)
- Weight problems (often overweight or obese)
- Lack of exercise
- Sexual dysfunction

Obesity. Most people with schizophrenia are overweight or obese, which may be because of a poor diet, lack of exercise, psychotropic medication (see below), or a combination of the three. Individuals with schizophrenia have a different pattern of obesity from that seen among the general population: their body mass index (BMI) rises through middle age and falls in later life, whereas in the general population BMI continues to rise with age. A raised BMI at any age and in both genders is associated with increased mortality,[8] but the combination of obesity with smoking presents a particularly potent risk for coronary heart disease.

Weight gain is probably the biggest risk factor for emergent diabetes in schizophrenia; type 2 diabetes is about 2–4 times more prevalent in people with schizophrenia than in the general population.[9] Obesity and type 2 diabetes are part of what is called the 'metabolic syndrome', which also includes insulin resistance, dyslipidemia and hypertension. This constellation of cardiovascular risk factors predisposes the schizophrenic patient to atheroma formation and increased risk of premature death from myocardial infarction or stroke.

Medication. Most people with schizophrenia take psychotropic medication for many years. Antipsychotic drugs are the most widely prescribed group, but antidepressants and anxiolytics are also often prescribed for considerable periods of time. Antipsychotics are implicated in obesity (see above) and may interact with other factors to cause QTC prolongation (observed by electrocardiography) and ventricular arrhythmias.

Sexual dysfunction, especially erectile dysfunction, in which antipsychotic drugs have been implicated, is common in individuals with schizophrenia.[10]

Specific approaches to improve physical health
Improving the physical health of individuals with schizophrenia is very difficult. The illness itself may hinder success: positive, negative and cognitive symptoms may all contribute. However, there are a number of specific approaches that can be employed (Table 2).

53

TABLE 2

Specific interventions to improve physical health in people with schizophrenia

- Smoking cessation
- Dietary changes
- Pharmacological treatment of erectile dysfunction

Lifestyle issues would seem the most obvious to tackle, but the results are not impressive.

Smoking cessation. Attempts to help patients stop smoking have met with variable success.[11] The first double-blind study of the noradrenaline- and dopamine-reuptake inhibitor bupropion for smoking cessation in individuals with schizophrenia found the drug to be modestly effective for smoking cessation without worsening the clinical symptoms of schizophrenia.[12]

Dietary changes. The findings of the first randomized controlled trial of dietary intervention in people with schizophrenia showed that, when given free fruit and vegetables for a period of six months, subjects consumed markedly more fruit and vegetables than control (treatment-as-usual) participants.[13] However, 12 months after the intervention stopped, consumption of fruit and vegetables fell back to pretreatment levels.

Medication. Also recently reported is the first randomized controlled trial of the phosphodiesterase type 5 inhibitor sildenafil in the treatment of erectile dysfunction in people with schizophrenia.[14] The trial was deemed a 'failure', as although 179 men were approached, only 24 consented to enter the study. It seemed that the men had little interest in improving their sexual functioning.

A question of responsibility

The specific approaches described above will improve the physical health of people with schizophrenia, but it needs to be clear who is responsible for the health of these individuals, apart from the people

Highlights in **the physical health of people with schizophrenia** 2005–06

WHAT'S IN?

- Recognition that the physical health of people with schizophrenia is poor

- Awareness that abnormalities of glucose metabolism in people with schizophrenia may in part be intimately related to the illness itself

- Modestly successful interventions to improve dietary habits and to help people with schizophrenia stop smoking

- Recognition that primary care services should not accept complete responsibility for regular and full assessment of the physical health of people with schizophrenia, but that the main responsibility should be with secondary care services, who have regular contact with individuals with schizophrenia

WHAT'S OUT?

- Statistics from earlier studies for deaths due to suicide in people with schizophrenia, which have now been found to be much lower than previously thought (i.e. 5%, not 10%)

themselves and their carers, who are often more concerned about their relative's health than the actual patient.[15] Primary care providers are now encouraged to take an interest in people with severe mental illness. In the UK, the General Medical Services contract offers financial incentives to general practitioners who register people with schizophrenia for regular physical health checks and advice on the side effects of long-term medication. However, evidence suggests that people with schizophrenia attend their general practitioner's surgery just as often as other people, if not more often.[16]

In general, secondary care services, such as the community mental health team, are the professionals who have the most contact with people with schizophrenia. Issues concerning both the physical and mental health of individuals with schizophrenia should be addressed by this group. In the UK, this is certainly the view of the National Institute for Health and Clinical Excellence, which states that 'secondary services should undertake regular and full assessment of the mental and physical health of service users'.[17] Advice on healthy eating, weight management, routine physical examination and annual blood monitoring (blood sugar, lipid, prolactin) are all recommended. Nevertheless, although some of the causes of ill health in individuals with schizophrenia are now well known, tackling them satisfactorily still appears to be a long way off.

References

1. Palmer BA, Pankratz VS, Bostwick JM. The lifetime risk of suicide in schizophrenia: a reexamination. *Arch Gen Psychiatry* 2005;62:247–53.

2. Jablensky A, Lawrence D. Schizophrenia and cancer: is there a need to invoke a protective gene? *Arch Gen Psychiatry* 2001;58: 579–80.

3. McCreadie RG, Stevens H, Henderson J et al. The dental health of people with schizophrenia. *Acta Psychiatr Scand* 2004;110:306–10.

4. Thakore JH, Mann JN, Vlahos I et al. Increased visceral fat distribution in drug-naive and drug-free patients with schizophrenia. *Int J Obes Relat Metab Disord* 2002;26:137–41.

5. Ryan MC, Collins P, Thakore JH. Impaired fasting glucose tolerance in first-episode, drug-naive patients with schizophrenia. *Am J Psychiatry* 2003;160:284–9.

6. Kelly C, McCreadie RG. Smoking habits, current symptoms, and premorbid characteristics of schizophrenic patients in Nithsdale, Scotland. *Am J Psychiatry* 1999;156:1751–7.

7. McCreadie RG; Scottish Schizophrenia Lifestyle Group. Diet, smoking and cardiovascular risk in people with schizophrenia: descriptive study. *Br J Psychiatry* 2003;183:534–9.

8. Calle EE, Thun MJ, Petrelli JM et al. Body-mass index and mortality in a prospective cohort of U.S. adults. *New Engl J Med* 1999;341: 1097–105.

9. Bushe C, Holt RIG. Prevalence of diabetes and impaired glucose tolerance in patients with schizophrenia. *Br J Psychiatry Suppl* 2004;47:S67–71.

10. Macdonald S, Halliday J, MacEwan T et al. The Nithsdale Schizophrenia Surveys 24: sexual dysfunction. Case-control study. *Br J Psychiatry* 2003;182:50–6.

11. Kelly C, McCreadie RG. Cigarette smoking and schizophrenia. *Adv Psychiatr Treat* 2000;6:327–31.

12. Evins AE, Cather C, Deckersbach T et al. A double-blind placebo-controlled trial of bupropion sustained-release for smoking cessation in schizophrenia. *J Clin Psychopharmacol* 2005;25:218–25.

13. McCreadie RG, Kelly C, Connolly M et al. Dietary improvement in people with schizophrenia: randomised controlled trial. *Br J Psychiatry* 2005;187: 346–51.

14. McCreadie RG, Stockton-Henderson J, Fisher H et al. Sildenafil in males with schizophrenia and erectile dysfunction: randomised controlled trial. *Q J Ment Health* 2006; in press.

15. Foldemo A, Ek AC, Bogren L. Needs in outpatients with schizophrenia, assessed by the patients themselves and their parents and staff. *Soc Psychiatry Psychiatr Epidemiol* 2004;39:381–5.

16. Osborn DP, King MB, Nazareth I. Participation in screening for cardiovascular risk by people with schizophrenia or similar mental illnesses: cross sectional study in general practice. *BMJ* 2003;326: 1122–3.

17. National Institute for Clinical Excellence. Schizophrenia. Core interventions in the treatment and management of schizophrenia in primary and secondary care. Clinical Guideline 1. London, UK: NICE, 2002. www.nice.org.uk/pdf/ CG1NICEguideline.pdf

Hans Schanda MD

Justizanstalt Göllersdorf, Göllersdorf; and Psychiatric University Clinic, Vienna, Austria

The unpredictable but cold and calculating murderer, acting along the lines of Stevenson's Dr Jekyll and Mr Hyde, is one of the most popular stereotypes of the mass and entertainment media. Likewise, severe incidents and high-profile killings committed by psychiatric patients confirm public prejudices concerning the outstanding level of danger that individuals with severe mental illness represent, in particular subjects with the colloquial epitome of severe mental illness – 'schizophrenia'.

However, the vivid description of stab wounds in the gutter press is hardly sufficient evidence on which to base a diagnosis of psychosis. More professional (and unemotional) criteria are needed to question the threat posed by subjects suffering from functional (schizophrenic, affective) psychoses, usually summarized under the term major mental disorders (MMD).

Current state of knowledge

Nearly all recent publications confirm a moderate but statistically significant association between MMD and criminal behavior in general.[1,2] The lower the rate of offending in a defined population, the more obvious the association (i.e. a higher risk in women than men,[3–5] and a higher risk of violent offences compared with criminality in general).[3,4,6,7] This association is particularly evident in homicide.

Table 1 shows the results of studies published since 1995, all of which report that individuals with schizophrenia have an increased likelihood of committing homicide of about eight- to tenfold in men and up to 18-fold in women (bearing in mind that, in general, women are less likely than men to commit violent crimes).[4,6,8–11] As in criminality in general, comorbid substance abuse considerably contributes to these figures.

TABLE 1

The main results of recent studies on homicide and major mental disorders

Country	Results
Eronen 1995[8]	
Finland	OR (95% CI):
	• Schizophrenia: W **10.8** (5.5–21.3); with comorbid alcoholism **77.0** (24.4–246.6), without comorbid alcoholism **7.4** (3.2–16.8)
	• Major depressive episode: W 2.0 (0.9–4.2)
	• Markedly higher risks in alcoholism and antisocial personality disorder
Eronen et al. 1996[9]	
Finland	OR (95% CI):
	• Schizophrenia: M **8.0** (6.1–10.4), W **6.5** (2.6–16.0)
	• Major depressive episode: M **1.6** (1.1–2.4), W 1.8 (0.7–4.4)
	• Higher risks in alcoholism and antisocial personality disorder
Eronen et al. 1996[10]	
Finland	OR (95% CI):
	• Schizophrenia: M **10.0** (8.1–12.5), W **8.7** (4.8–18.7); with comorbid alcoholism M **17.2** (12.4–23.7), W **80.9** (25.7–255.0); without comorbid alcoholism M **7.3** (5.4–9.7), W **5.1** (1.9–13.7)
Wallace et al. 1998[11]	
Australia	OR (95% CI):
	• Schizophrenia: M **10.1** (5.5–18.6), W **10.6** (1.4–80.4)
	• Affective psychoses: M **5.0** (1.3–20.9), W **16.9** (2.2–127.7)

(CONTINUED)

TABLE 1 (CONTINUED)

Country   Results

Taylor & Gunn 1999[20]

England   • Little fluctuation of mentally disordered offenders
          (i.e. not guilty by reason of insanity, unfit to plead)
          between 1957 and 1995

Erb et al. 2001[6]

Germany   OR (95% CI):

          • Schizophrenia: M+W (1955–1964) **12.7** (11.2–14.3);
            (1992–1996) **16.6** (11.2–24.5)

          • Statistically significant increase of comorbid alcohol
            abuse/dependence, previous offences and previous
            violent offences

Schanda et al. 2004[4]

Austria   OR (95% CI):

          • Schizophrenia: M+W **8.8** (6.7–11.5), M **5.9** (4.3–8.0),
            W **18.8** (11.2–31.6); with comorbid alcoholism
            M+W **20.7** (12.4–34.1); without comorbid
            alcoholism M+W **7.1** (5.1–9.8)

          • Major depressive episode: M 0.4 (0.2–0.9),
            W 1.9 (0.9–4.1)

          • Affective psychoses: M 0.6 (0.3–1.0); with comorbid
            alcoholism M+W **3.1** (1.3–7.2); without comorbid
            alcoholism M+W 0.4 (0.2–0.7)

Simpson et al. 2004[5]

New   • 8.7% of all homicide offenders between 1970 and
Zealand   2000 were found to be 'mentally abnormal' (unfit
            to plead, not guilty by reason of insanity), most of
            them suffering from schizophrenia

          • Percentage of 'mentally abnormal homicide'
            reduced from the first 5 years to the last 5 years
            of the study

CI, confidence interval; M, men; OR, odds ratio; W, women.
Statistically significant results are in bold.

Although there is an independent, statistically significant increased risk associated with 'pure' schizophrenia,[4,8,10] homicide remains a rather rare event among patients suffering from schizophrenia[1,2,8,9,12,13] when compared with individuals with a problem of substance abuse or with (antisocial) personality disorders.

Only four studies provide data on affective psychoses. In three of them, the likelihood of homicide does not exceed that in the general population.[4,8,9] Even when there is comorbid alcoholism the results scarcely reach statistical significance.[4] The data of the Australian study seemingly point to a markedly increased likelihood of homicide in patients with affective psychoses.[11] However, the risk figures are flawed by statistical problems due to a limited number of cases, and, therefore, are not convincing.[2]

The offenders and their victims

Against all common prejudices, it is not 'the schizophrenic' who is dangerous. The figures reported above have to be primarily ascribed to the activities of a small subgroup of patients with certain clinical features, including:

- florid (and often untreated) delusional symptoms[1,10,14,15]
- high rates of comorbid substance abuse and (antisocial) personality disorders[1,4,6,16]
- lack of insight and compliance and, therefore, non-adherence to medication.[17]

As all recent studies have confirmed, severely mentally ill patients who exhibit homicidal behavior primarily attack people with whom they have close (and often ambivalent and highly emotional) relationships. The victims of schizophrenic homicide offenders mostly stem from the patients' immediate environment.[5,12,13,15,18] However, patients with additional (comorbid) antisocial personality disorder have been shown to assault non-relatives more frequently. Such offenders are less likely to be driven by psychotic symptoms, but instead may be involved in an altercation with their subsequent victim. They also exhibit higher rates of comorbid alcoholism.[15] These findings concur with the observation that the greater influence of general criminogenic factors on violent behavior in mentally ill subjects is associated with a greater probability that such patients will attack strangers.

Community care and homicidal behavior

During the past decades we have been confronted with fundamental changes in general mental healthcare. Since the introduction of psychiatry reforms, the majority of severely mentally ill patients spend their lives out of hospital. As every European country is reporting rapidly growing admission rates of mentally ill offenders to forensic hospitals,[19] it would be fair to assume that modern community care poses an increased risk to society. Only a few longitudinal studies are able to evaluate whether this is, indeed, the case (Table 1).

Taylor and Gunn found no increase in the proportion of people with mental illness among all homicide offenders in England during a 38-year period.[20] Erb et al. compared German data from the late 1950s and early 1960s with recent data from Hessen (Germany), and came to the same conclusion; there was no statistically significant increase in the proportion of homicide offenders with schizophrenia over time.[6] However, some characteristics of the offender populations had changed. The authors found statistically significant higher rates of comorbid alcohol abuse/dependence, previous offences and previous violent offences in the post-reform sample. A recently published study from New Zealand reported a decline in the quota of 'mentally abnormal' homicide offenders between 1970 and 2000.[5]

Are public fears justified?

According to current knowledge, we have to accept that individuals with MMD are more likely to commit acts of severe violence than the general population. This nearly exclusively concerns patients with schizophrenia. Mental health professionals are ill-advised to believe that denial of this fact could protect their patients from old, deep-rooted prejudices. A reality-based, balanced view may help to solve this apparent dilemma.

To correctly appraise the danger individuals with MMD pose to society, we first have to examine the uniform, robust and statistically significant findings of all respective studies. Such research shows that the probability of individuals with MMD committing homicide is low compared with that of subjects with substance-abuse problems and (antisocial) personality disorders.[1,2,8,9,12,13] Therefore, the suggestion made by Walsh et al. – to focus public debate on the relative percentage risk attributable to a certain mental condition in terms of the total amount of violence in society – cannot be dismissed as a mathematical trick covering up an unpleasant reality.[1] When the population-attributable (relative) risk is calculated, about 5% of all homicide offenders are found to have a life-time diagnosis of schizophrenia.[21] Applying this method to the basic data of a recently published study on homicide, only 4.2% of all homicides could be ascribed to MMD.[4] This figure roughly represents the gain in public security if MMD did not exist. It should certainly not support public fears or provide an authorization for restrictive measures against 'the mentally ill' in general.

Moreover, relative risk is a measure of association, not causation. It tells us nothing about the complicated and differing pathways leading to violence.[4,15] For example, delusions are common in schizophrenia, but only a small minority of patients exhibit severe, delusionally driven violence. Therefore, other mechanisms must be operating.[14,22] This could explain the divergent results of studies on the influence of certain psychotic symptoms on violent behavior.[14,23,24]

The finding that community mental healthcare did not lead to an increase in homicide among the mentally ill[5,6,20] confirms the conviction of some mental health professionals that treatment cannot substantially influence the amount of violent behavior exhibited by their patients. This is not true. The actions of mental health professionals in the run-up to fatal incidents are often found to be inadequate, and they cannot be released from responsibility.[25] Likewise, the steadily increasing rates of admissions to forensic hospitals cannot be solely ascribed to factors such as bed closure or restrictive criteria for involuntary hospital admission.[19,26]

Highlights in major mental disorders and homicide 2005–06

WHAT'S IN?

- An awareness that, compared with the general population, patients with major mental disorders (MMD) – primarily schizophrenia – are more likely to commit homicide

- An awareness that the probability of individuals with schizophrenia committing homicide is considerably lower than that of individuals with substance-abuse problems and (antisocial) personality disorders

- Recognition that patients at higher risk are characterized by severe, chronic course, florid psychotic symptoms, lack of insight and compliance, and higher rates of comorbid substance abuse

- An awareness that homicide victims mainly stem from the patients' close environment

WHAT'S OUT?

- The perception that if patients with MMD commit homicidal acts it has to be solely ascribed to general criminogenic factors such as substance abuse and (antisocial) personality disorders

- The belief that patients with MMD living in the community pose a menace to society

WHAT'S NEEDED?

- Awareness of the above-mentioned issues among mental health professionals and politicians

- A rational, unemotional view of the deficits of community mental healthcare

- Adequate and consequent long-term treatment, especially for the most severely mentally ill patients

Aside from suicide prophylaxis, the prevention of dangerous and violent behavior in mentally ill patients is a task for the psychiatric profession. To be aware of this fact represents an undeniable basis for the provision of adequate treatment for all severely mentally ill subjects.

References

1. Walsh E, Buchanan A, Fahy T. Violence and schizophrenia: examining the evidence. *Br J Psychiatry* 2002;180:490–5.

2. Schanda H. Investigating the association between psychosis and criminality/violence [in German]. *Fortschr Neurol Psychiatr* 2006; 74:85–100.

3. Hodgins S, Mednick SA, Brennan PA et al. Mental disorder and crime: evidence from a Danish birth cohort. *Arch Gen Psychiatry* 1996;53: 489–96.

4. Schanda H, Knecht G, Schreinzer D et al. Homicide and major mental disorders: a 25-year study. *Acta Psychiatr Scand* 2004;110: 98–107.

5. Simpson AI, McKenna B, Moskowitz A et al. Homicide and mental illness in New Zealand, 1970–2000. *Br J Psychiatry* 2004;185:394–8.

6. Erb M, Hodgins S, Freese R et al. Homicide and schizophrenia: maybe treatment does have a preventive effect. *Crim Behav Ment Health* 2001;11:6–26.

7. Wallace C, Mullen PE, Burgess P. Criminal offending in schizophrenia over a 25-year period marked by deinstitutionalization and increasing prevalence of comorbid substance use disorders. *Am J Psychiatry* 2004;161: 716–27.

8. Eronen M. Mental disorders and homicidal behavior in female subjects. *Am J Psychiatry* 1995; 152:1216–18.

9. Eronen M, Hakola P, Tiihonen J. Mental disorders and homicidal behavior in Finland. *Arch Gen Psychiatry* 1996;53:497–501.

10. Eronen M, Tiihonen J, Hakola P. Schizophrenia and homicidal behavior. *Schizophr Bull* 1996;22: 83–9.

11. Wallace C, Mullen P, Burgess P et al. Serious criminal offending and mental disorder. Case linkage study. *Br J Psychiatry* 1998;172: 477–84.

12. Shaw J, Appleby L, Amos T et al. Mental disorder and clinical care in people convicted of homicide: national clinical survey. *BMJ* 1999;318:1240–4.

13. Shaw J, Amos T, Hunt IM et al. Mental illness in people who kill strangers: longitudinal study and national clinical survey. *BMJ* 2004;328:734–7.

14. Taylor PJ, Leese M, Williams D et al. Mental disorder and violence. A special (high security) hospital study. *Br J Psychiatry* 1998;172:218–26.

15. Joyal CC, Putkonen P, Paavola P, Tiihonen J. Characteristics and circumstances of homicidal acts committed by offenders with schizophrenia. *Psychol Med* 2004; 34:433–42.

16. Putkonen A, Kotilainen I, Joyal CC, Tiihonen J. Comorbid personality disorders and substance use disorders of mentally ill homicide offenders: a structured clinical study on dual and triple diagnoses. *Schizophr Bull* 2004;30:59–72.

17. Swartz MS, Swanson JW, Hiday VA et al. Violence and severe mental illness: the effects of substance abuse and nonadherence to medication. *Am J Psychiatry* 1998;155:226–31.

18. Nordström A, Kullgren G. Victim relations and victim gender in violent crimes committed by offenders with schizophrenia. *Soc Psychiatry Psychiatr Epidemiol* 2003;38: 326–30.

19. Priebe S, Badesconyi A, Fioritti A et al. Reinstitutionalisation in mental health care: comparison of data on service provision from six European countries. *BMJ* 2005;330:123–6.

20. Taylor PJ, Gunn J. Homicides by people with mental illness: myth and reality. *Br J Psychiatry* 1999;174: 9–14.

21. Walsh E, Fahy T. Violence in society. *BMJ* 2002;325:507–8.

22. Schanda H. Psychiatry reforms and illegal behaviour of the severely mentally ill. *Lancet* 2005;365:367–9.

23. Appelbaum PS, Robbins PC, Monahan J. Violence and delusions: data from the MacArthur Violence Risk Assessment Study. *Am J Psychiatry* 2000;157:566–72.

24. Stompe T, Ortwein-Swoboda G, Schanda H. Schizophrenia, delusional symptoms and violence: the threat/control override concept reexamined. *Schizophr Bull* 2004; 30:31–44.

25. Gunn J. Let's get serious about dangerousness. *Crim Behav Ment Health* 1996; Suppl:51–64.

26. Schanda H, Stompe T. Psychiatry reform, coercive treatment and violence: developments in Austrian mental health care. *Eur Psychiatry* 2004;19(suppl 1):30S–1S.

Benzodiazepine use and cognitive decline

Hélène Verdoux MD PhD, Rajaa Lagnaoui PharmD PhD,
Bernard Bégaud MD PhD
Université Victor Ségalen Bordeaux2, INSERM U657, Bordeaux, France

Although the therapeutic benefits of benzodiazepines are undisputed, adverse effects such as dependence and withdrawal syndrome are also well identified.[1,2] The negative effect of benzodiazepines on cognitive performance, particularly on memory, is well documented by a large body of evidence.[3] The decision to prescribe benzodiazepines is usually made after considering both the risks and benefits associated with the contemporary use of these drugs. However, the risk–benefit assessment should also take into account delayed adverse effects.

Few studies have explored the long-term effect of benzodiazepine exposure on cognitive performance, and whether or not cognitive deficits persist after withdrawal.[4,5] This issue is nevertheless of great interest from a public health point of view, since a large percentage of the adult and elderly population is exposed to benzodiazepines in most developed countries.

Cognitive deficits associated with problematic benzodiazepine use

The persistence of cognitive deficits after withdrawal from long-term benzodiazepine use was recently addressed in a meta-analysis of nine studies published between 1980 and 2000.[6] All studies involved subjects with at least 1 year of benzodiazepine use (mean length of 9 years), and the clinical samples included patients recruited in hospital settings for benzodiazepine withdrawal or for investigation of drug dependence.

Seven studies used a control group (normal controls in six studies; subjects with anxiety disorder in one study), and the other two studies used cognitive norms. The use of alcohol and other medication was documented in most studies.

Cognitive assessment was performed at baseline and repeated at a median of 3 months after withdrawal. The various types of cognitive measures were combined into 12 cognitive categories; the cognitive domain most frequently measured was attention/concentration. Compared with controls or norms, former benzodiazepine users had poorer performance in all cognitive categories, except sensory processing. The strongest impairment (as measured by the effect size) was found in subjects' verbal memory.

In a recent study not included in this meta-analysis, Barker and colleagues explored neuropsychological performances in 20 chronic benzodiazepine users (with a mean duration of exposure of 108 months). All of the subjects had successfully withdrawn from these drugs for more than 6 months (mean of 42 months).[7] Compared with control subjects with and without anxiety disorders, all of whom had never used benzodiazepines, former benzodiazepine users demonstrated greater impairment in tests for verbal and non-verbal memory and motor/control activities, but not for visuospatial skills and attention/concentration.

Unfortunately, it is difficult to generalize for the whole population of benzodiazepine users on the basis of these findings alone. These studies included patients with problematic benzodiazepine use, who required specialized treatment, and therefore the data were concentrated on highly selected populations of benzodiazepine users who were more likely to have been exposed to benzodiazepines for longer durations and/or at higher dosages. Furthermore, only subjects with successful withdrawal were considered.

In addition, these studies did not demonstrate whether any of the cognitive deficits existed before the use of benzodiazepines, or whether they were de novo deficits with onset during, or after long-term, benzodiazepine exposure. Nevertheless, these studies do provide detailed information on the history of benzodiazepine use, and extensive neuropsychological assessment.

Cognitive decline associated with general benzodiazepine use

Prospective studies of unselected subjects from the general population may provide answers to questions that remain unsolved by studies performed in clinical samples.

Six studies carried out over the past decade on prospective cohorts of elderly subjects from the general population have explored whether chronic exposure to benzodiazepines was associated with an increased risk of incident cognitive decline. The methods and results are shown in Table 1.

Notably, three of the studies were carried out in France, perhaps because of the wide use of these psychotropic drugs in this country.

In all studies, benzodiazepine users were compared with subjects who had never used benzodiazepines and who continued not to use them throughout the follow-up periods involved.

One study reported a 'protective' effect of benzodiazepines on the risk of dementia.[8] However, the lack of distinction between subjects exposed to benzodiazepines at baseline and those exposed at each follow-up assessment may have introduced a spurious association, since benzodiazepine use may have been stopped in subjects with incipient dementia. Hence, those who were still using benzodiazepines at the end of the follow-up period had a lower risk of dementia.[9]

Another study reported that subjects using benzodiazepines only at the baseline assessment had a lower risk of cognitive decline.[10]

Two studies found no association between benzodiazepine use and cognitive decline.[11,12]

Three of the studies reported that benzodiazepine users had an increased risk of cognitive decline, although this risk was restricted to categories of users that differed from one study to another: new users, but not chronic or former users;[10] former users, but not current users at the time of diagnosis of dementia;[9] chronic users, but not occasional users.[13] These discrepancies may be explained by the different methodologies used in each study.

69

TABLE 1

Prospective cohort studies exploring the association between exposure to benzodiazepines and cognitive decline

	Population	Selection
EPESE study New Haven site, NC, USA[10]	• 1200 subjects • ≥ 65 years • non-institutionalized	Random, using stratified household sampling
EPESE study Duke site, NC, USA[12]	• 2765 subjects • ≥ 65 years • non-institutionalized	Random, using stratified household sampling; self-respondent
Kungsholmen study Sweden[8]	• 242 subjects • MMSE ≥ 23 at inclusion • ≥ 75 years	Random, from subjects registered in a parish of Stockholm
PAQUID study France[9]	• ≥ 65 years • non-institutionalized • nested case-control design: 150 cases of incident dementia over the follow-up • 3159 controls without dementia at index date (time of diagnosis of the cases)	Recruited using electoral rolls

Follow-up	Benzodiazepine exposure	Main findings
2 assessments at baseline (1982) and after 6 years (1988)	Prescribed medication used for past 2 weeks *Type of users:* • non-consumers (90.4%) (baseline) • continuous (T1, T2) (2.2%) • temporary (T1) (3.9%) • new (T2) (3.5%)	• Decreased risk of cognitive decline in 'temporary' users (OR = 0.2) • Increased risk (NS) of cognitive decline in new users (OR = 2)
2 assessments at baseline (1986–87) and after 3 years (1989–90)	Prescribed medication used for past 2 weeks *Type of users:* • non-users (85.8%) (baseline) • current (T2) (9.5%) • previous (T1) (4.7%)	• Previous and curent use not associated with cognitive decline
2 assessments at baseline (1987) and after 3 years (1990)	Regular and 'as needed' for 2 previous weeks *Type of users:* • T1 or T2 (30%)	• Incidence of DSM-III-R dementia significantly lower in users (9%) than non-users (23%)
4 assessments at baseline (1989), with follow-up at 3, 5 and 8 years (1997)	Spontaneous reporting of prescribed and non-prescribed medication used in past 2 weeks. *Type of users:* • non-users (35.3% cases; 51.3% controls) • current: use at index date (34.3% cases; 33.2% controls) • former: use ended 2–3 years before index date (12.9% cases; 6.3% controls)	• Former use (OR = 2.3) associated with increased risk of dementia • No association between current use and risk of dementia

(CONTINUED)

TABLE 1 (CONTINUED)

	Population	Selection
EVA study France[13]	• 1176 subjects • 60–70 years • non-institutionalized	Volunteers, recruited using electoral rolls
Eugeria study France[11]	• 372 subjects • mean 76 years • unknown proportion of institutionalized subjects	

Adapted from Verdoux et al.[5]
EPESE, Established Population for Epidemiological Studies of the Elderly;
EVA, Epidemiology of Vascular Aging; MMSE, Mini-Mental State Examination;
NS, Not significant; PAQUID, Personnes Agées QUID.
T1, T2, Tn: 1st, 2nd, nth assessment.

The differences in methodology between these studies include variation in:

• the definition of benzodiazepine exposure
• the duration of follow-up
• the measure and definition of cognitive decline (differences in performance on cognitive tests between baseline and follow-up assessments, or onset of DSM-III-R dementia).

In all studies, the analyses were adjusted for potential confounding factors, but not all of them explored the effect of psychiatric status, or the effects of alcohol use and other psychotropic medications.

Follow-up	Benzodiazepine exposure	Main findings
3 assessments at baseline (1991–93), and after 2 and 4 years (1995–97)	All drugs regularly used last month from medical prescription *Type of users:* • non-consumers (77.6%) • chronic (T1, T2, T3) (7%) • episodic (1 of the 3 assessments) (10%) • recurrent (2 assessments) (6%)	• Cognitive decline twice as likely in chronic users as in non-users • Episodic or recurrent use not associated with cognitive decline
3 assessments at baseline, and after 1 and 2 years	Inspection of medication and prescription; no time range defined *Type of users:* • non-consumers (65.9%) • chronic (T1, T3) (7.5%)	• No association between chronic use and cognitive decline (estimate not given; strength and direction of the association unknown)

Limitations of studies to date

The strengths and limitations of these epidemiological studies mirror those of studies carried out on clinical samples: the subjects were unselected and cognitive decline was prospectively assessed, but only cross-sectional measures of benzodiazepine use at each assessment were available. Hence no information was collected on the total duration of exposure to benzodiazepines and on the exact duration of withdrawal for former users.

It is also unknown whether benzodiazepines increase the risk of cognitive decline only by interacting with a pre-existing vulnerability.

Despite these limitations, there is converging evidence from clinical and epidemiological studies that chronic use of benzodiazepines may induce cognitive deficits that persist after withdrawal.

Although these findings need to be confirmed by further studies, they strongly support the recommendation to avoid long-term prescription of benzodiazepines in elderly subjects, and to drastically limit prescription in younger subjects.

Highlights *in* **benzodiazepine use and cognitive decline** *2005–06*

WHAT'S IN?

- Recognition that cognitive deficits persist in chronic benzodiazepine users several months after successful withdrawal

- Awareness that exposure to benzodiazepines may increase the risk of cognitive decline in elderly subjects within the community

WHAT'S NEEDED?

- Research to explore whether there is a dose–response relationship between lifetime exposure to benzodiazepines and cognitive decline

- Identification of the neurobiological mechanisms underlying the putative link between chronic benzodiazepine use and cognitive decline

- Better evaluation of whether the link between benzodiazepines and cognitive decline is confounded by the psychopathological status of chronic benzodiazepine users

- Pharmacoepidemiological studies in population-based samples of elderly subjects, but also of young and middle-aged adults

- Constraint in the prescription of long-term benzodiazepine use

References

1. Lader M. Drug treatment of generalized anxiety disorder. In: *Psychiatry Highlights 2003–04.* Oxford: Health Press, 2004:43–50.

2. Lader M. Benzodiazepines. A risk-benefit profile. *CNS Drugs* 1994;1:377–87.

3. Curran HV. Benzodiazepines, memory and mood: a review. *Psychopharmacology (Berl)* 1991;105:1–8.

4. Stewart SA. The effects of benzodiazepines on cognition. *J Clin Psychiatry* 2005;66(suppl 2):9–13.

5. Verdoux H, Lagnaoui R, Bégaud B. Is benzodiazepine use a risk factor for cognitive decline and dementia? A literature review of epidemiological studies. *Psychol Med* 2005;35:307–15.

6. Barker MJ, Greenwood KM, Jackson M, Crowe SF. Persistence of cognitive effects after withdrawal from long-term benzodiazepine use: a meta-analysis. *Arch Clin Neuropsychol* 2004;19:437–54.

7. Barker MJ, Greenwood KM, Jackson M, Crowe SF. An evaluation of persisting cognitive effects after withdrawal from long-term benzodiazepine use. *J Int Neuropsychol Soc* 2005;11:281–9.

8. Fastbom J, Forsell Y, Winblad B. Benzodiazepines may have protective effects against Alzheimer disease. *Alzheimer Dis Assoc Disord* 1998; 12:14–17.

9. Lagnaoui R, Bégaud B, Moore N et al. Benzodiazepine use and risk of dementia: a nested case-control study. *J Clin Epidemiol* 2002;55:314–18.

10. Dealberto MJ, Mcavay GJ, Seeman T, Berkman L. Psychotropic drug use and cognitive decline among older men and women. *Int J Geriatr Psychiatry* 1997;12:567–74.

11. Allard J, Artero S, Ritchie K. Consumption of psychotropic medication in the elderly: a re-evaluation of its effect on cognitive performance. *Int J Geriatr Psychiatry* 2003;18:874–8.

12. Hanlon JT, Horner RD, Schmader KE et al. Benzodiazepine use and cognitive function among community-dwelling elderly. *Clin Pharmacol Ther* 1998;64:684–92.

13. Paterniti S, Dufouil C, Alperovitch A. Long-term benzodiazepine use and cognitive decline in the elderly: the Epidemiology of Vascular Aging Study. *J Clin Psychopharmacol* 2002;22:285–93.

Szabolcs Kéri MD PhD

Department of Psychiatry, University of Szeged, Szeged, Hungary

The term 'theory of mind' (ToM) refers to our ability to interpret and predict other people's intentions, wishes, thoughts and feelings and to explain their behavior in terms of these mental states.[1] This type of reasoning is fundamentally different from that used to explain the causal relationships of the physical world. Psychologists often call ToM and related functions 'folk psychology' or 'intuitive psychology' in order to illustrate its naturalness and spontaneity. Folk psychology describes our cognitive capacity to interpret inner states of minds, whereas 'folk physics' and 'folk biology' are related to the mechanical and animate world, respectively.[2]

The 'mindblindness' of autism

ToM can be explained using descriptive stories or series of cartoons. For example, in the famous 'Sally and Ann' false belief task, Sally has a marble, which she places in a basket and covers. When Sally is not in the room, Ann removes the marble from the basket and places it in a box. So where will Sally look for the marble? To predict Sally's behavior, her belief concerning the location of the marble must be taken into account rather than the physical reality. Healthy children over 4 years of age are able to successfully answer the question by recognizing Sally's false belief that the marble is still in the basket. However, children with autism show severe deficits that cannot be explained by a lower IQ.[3] In this situation, they cannot appreciate that Sally's belief would differ from their own. Similarly, people with autism fail to recognize complex mental states from expressions in the eye region.

Patients who pass first-order ToM tasks, during which they must interpret the mental states of other people in response to real events, can still show deficits on second-order ToM tasks, which require an understanding of what other people are thinking (about the thoughts of others). Impaired ToM may lead to deficits in social behavior, imagination and communication. For example, people with autism are less able to take into consideration the expectations and background knowledge of others during conversations, and to detect when something is said that the other person should not know about (faux pas).[3]

Is there a special neuronal circuitry involved?

Functional neuroimaging studies have revealed that several brain areas are specifically activated during various ToM tasks.[4] The anterior paracingulate cortex may be involved in the interpretation of mental states by decoupling beliefs and imaginary circumstances from physical reality, as illustrated by the 'Sally and Ann' story. The superior temporal cortex is important in the detection of biological motion, facial expression and body gestures. People routinely attribute intentions to objects that display biological motion, and the decoding of 'body language' is extremely important in order to correctly predict another person's mental state. Finally, the amygdala plays a crucial role in the recognition of emotional expressions, particularly complex social emotions, which are closely related to ToM functions.[4]

Theory of mind and schizophrenia

During the past decade, more than 60 papers have been published on ToM functions in schizophrenia.[5,6] It was postulated that, in addition to autistic withdrawal and social dysfunctions, psychotic symptoms might be a consequence of misrepresenting one's own intentions and misreading the intentions of others. Patients with schizophrenia may interpret beliefs as reality, which may lead to delusions. The impaired processing of social signals, intentions and indirect aspects of speech (i.e. when the speaker's real intentions differ from what they say) may result in communication problems and formal thought disorder.

Alternatively, ToM dysfunctions may be related to executive deficits (i.e. problems with functions such as selective attention, planning, impulse control and problem solving). Schizophrenia patients with disorganization symptoms show severe difficulties with ToM tasks, probably because they are not able to monitor their own actions, to interpret the mental states of others, or to integrate contextual information.

Recent evidence suggests that ToM dysfunctions correlate with abnormalities of motion perception, indicating that the ToM network is disrupted at an early stage of information processing.[7] Others suggest structural and functional abnormalities of the paracingulate region and amygdala.[8]

Less symptomatic patients also show ToM deficits in experimental situations. However, individuals with schizophrenia do not display severe ToM dysfunctions during real interpersonal interactions in clinical settings,[9] and delusions cannot be explained purely on the basis of ToM dysfunctions. Externalizing negative events and a tendency to blame others rather than circumstances are crucial factors in the development of persecutory delusions. ToM problems contribute to poor insight by disrupting the ability to understand other perspectives and to critically evaluate beliefs and circumstances.[10]

Theory of mind and mood disorders

ToM dysfunctions can be detected in mood disorders.[11–13] Depressed and manic patients with bipolar disorder display impaired performances in first-order and second-order ToM tasks.[11] Euthymic bipolar patients still show deficits but only on advanced ToM tests, such as recognizing complex mental states from expressions in the eye region of faces and deducing the real intentions behind indirect speech utterances. However, these residual disabilities may be because of an inability to recognize basic emotions, or because of executive dysfunctions.[12]

Women with unipolar major depressive disorder have significant difficulty in identifying mental states from expressions in the eye region. The ToM deficit shows a stronger relationship with affective, rather than somatic, symptoms of depression and does not seem to be influenced by anxiety.[13]

Highlights in **what is 'theory of mind'?** *2005–06*

WHAT'S IN?

- Theory of mind (ToM) as a common conceptual background for psychopathology, psychotherapy and clinical neuroscience
- An awareness that ToM dysfunctions contribute to several clinical symptoms, including social withdrawal, language disturbances and delusions
- Research that relates ToM to specialized brain areas

WHAT'S OUT?

- Popular misconceptions that the deficit of ToM is specific to autism, that ToM dysfunctions are a consequence of general intellectual disabilities and that ToM dysfunctions always lead to paranoid delusions

Finally, it has been hypothesized that ToM dysfunctions may account for various aspects of personality disorders, including antisocial, narcissistic and schizoid traits.[14] In this respect, more experimental evidence is warranted.

The value of theory of mind in psychiatry

Initially, ToM dysfunctions were thought to represent the specific cognitive mechanism of autism. However, evidence suggests that these deficits can be detected in various neuropsychiatric conditions. Some researchers are dubious as to how ToM dysfunctions contribute to behavioral and subjective symptoms and how they relate to other cognitive domains such as executive functions.

Despite these shortcomings, the concept of ToM may have a heuristic value in psychiatry, by introducing possible new concepts of evolutionary and developmental psychology and providing links between psychopathology, psychotherapy and clinical neuroscience.

From a clinical point of view, it is especially important to explore how systematic training for ToM functions could reduce certain dimensions of psychiatric symptoms to improve the psychosocial reintegration of patients living with severe mental disorders.

References

1. Premack D, Woodruff G. Does the chimpanzee have a theory of mind? *Behav Brain Sci* 1978;4:515–26.

2. Dennett DC. *The Intentional Stance*. Cambridge, Massachusetts: MIT Press, 1987.

3. Baron-Cohen S. The cognitive neuroscience of autism: evolutionary approaches. In: Gazzaniga MS, ed. *The New Cognitive Neurosciences*, 2nd edn. Cambridge, Massachusetts: MIT Press, 2000:1249–58.

4. Gallagher HL, Frith CD. Functional imaging of 'theory of mind'. *Trends Cogn Sci* 2003;7:77–83.

5. Frith CD. Schizophrenia and theory of mind. *Psychol Med* 2004;34:385–9.

6. Brune M. "Theory of mind" in schizophrenia: a review of the literature. *Schizophr Bull* 2005;31:21–42.

7. Kelemen O, Erdélyi R, Pataki I et al. Theory of mind and motion perception in schizophrenia. *Neuropsychology* 2005;19:494–500.

8. Suzuki M, Zhou SY, Hagino H et al. Morphological brain changes associated with Schneider's first-rank symptoms in schizophrenia: a MRI study. *Psychol Med* 2005;35:549–60.

9. McCabe R, Leudar I, Antaki C. Do people with schizophrenia display theory of mind deficits in clinical interactions? *Psychol Med* 2004;34:401–12.

10. Langdon R, Corner T, McLaren J et al. Externalizing and personalizing biases in persecutory delusions: The relationship with poor insight and theory-of-mind. *Behav Res Ther* 2005 Jul 20; [Epub ahead of print].

11. Kerr N, Dunbar RI, Bentall RP. Theory of mind deficits in bipolar affective disorder. *J Affect Disord* 2003;73:253–9.

12. Bora E, Vahip S, Gonul AS et al. Evidence for theory of mind deficits in euthymic patients with bipolar disorder. *Acta Psychiatr Scand* 2005;112:110–16.

13. Lee L, Harkness KL, Sabbagh MA, Jacobson JA. Mental state decoding abilities in clinical depression. *J Affect Disord* 2005;86:247–58.

14. Gabbard GO. Mind, brain, and personality disorders. *Am J Psychiatry* 2005;162:648–55.